THE ACHIEVEMENT
OF JOHN C. BENNETT

THE ACHIEVEMENT
OF JOHN C. BENNETT

David H. Smith

HERDER AND HERDER

1970
HERDER AND HERDER NEW YORK
232 Madison Avenue, New York 10016

CONTENTS

FOR MARIE-LOUISE

ABBREVIATIONS

SS	*Social Salvation* (1935)
CAOW	*Christianity—And Our World* (1936)
CR	*Christian Realism* (1941)
CESP	*Christian Ethics and Social Policy* (1946)
CCT	*Christianity and Communism* (1948)*
CC	*The Christian as Citizen* (1955)
CS	*Christians and the State* (1958)
WCMPD	*When Christians Make Political Decisions* (1954)
FPCP	*Foreign Policy in Christian Perspective* (1966)

* This book was revised in 1960, 1962, and again in 1969. The most recent version is called *Christianity and Communism Today*.

PREFACE

The writings of John Coleman Bennett, the current president of Union Theological Seminary in New York City, are important for two types of reasons. Historically, Bennett has been at the forefront of the movement to restructure American social Christianity. Although in the public eye he has always been overshadowed by Reinhold Niebuhr, Bennett's contributions in writing (beginning with *Social Salvation* in 1935) and organization (notably in the ecumenical movement) have been quantitatively vast and qualitatively distinctive. Thus an appraisal of recent Protestant social theory must come to terms with Bennett's thought.

The second complex of reasons which makes Bennett's work interesting is logical or philosophical. His writings are not primarily part of the past; he argues today for a certain understanding of the proper social role of religion and a religious body. The validity of his theory must be assessed; its merits must be fairly presented.

Bennett was born in 1902, the son of a Presbyterian minister. He grew up in Morristown, New Jersey, and attended Phillips Exeter Academy and Williams College. After graduation from Williams, Bennett went to theological school at Mansfield College, Oxford. He returned to this country and studied for the S.T.M. degree at Union Theological Seminary. At Union he met Reinhold Niebuhr—although Niebuhr was not Bennett's teacher in the formal sense of that word. During the 1930's Bennett taught at Auburn Theological Seminary and then (from 1938 to 1943) at the Pacific School of Religion. He was ordained to the Congregational ministry in 1939. In 1943 Bennett returned to Union and he has taught there ever since—interestingly enough, not so much Christian ethics as philosophical or systematic theology.

Early in his career Bennett characterized himself as "a liberal who tries to take seriously the contribution of such thinkers as Barth, Brunner and Reinhold Niebuhr and . . . a Congregationalist who believes in the central importance of the ecumenical Church,"[1] and the aptness of this will become apparent in the body of the book. At this point some attempt to characterize Bennett's overall style may be made. Bennett's articles and books are inevitably beautifully written and understated pieces, beginning with an introduction, including an enumeration of major points, and concluding with a brief summary. If sometimes Bennett's lists get out of hand, that is a small price to pay for the clarity of his writing. His style is witty ("the British people are really the most self-critical people on earth, at least when they are away from home"),[2] moderate (he is always against fury or frenzy), tasteful,[3] and often eloquent (for example, Billy Graham's visit to Union was "a very good lesson for us. It may have helped us to realize more vividly, what we should have known from Church history, that God can work powerfully through men who do not meet all our specifications.").[4] These gifts have placed Bennett's pen in great demand; his own characterization of William Temple fits its author rather well:

He is an irenic thinker with a vigorous point of view of his own. He has achieved extraordinary breadth of mind without sacrificing

---

[1] Bennett, *Christian Realism* (New York, 1941), p. ix.

[2] Bennett, "American Criticism of Britain" in *Christianity and Crisis,* IV, No. 24 (January 22, 1945), p. 6.

[3] As a marvelous example see "Mr. Dulles' Illness" in *Christianity and Crisis,* XIX, No. 4 (March 16, 1959), pp. 26–27.

[4] Bennett, "Billy Graham at Union" in *The Union Seminary Quarterly Review,* IX, No. 4 (May, 1954), p. 14.

consistency and incisiveness. For this reason, also, he is fitted by the qualities of his mind to be the leader of the Ecumenical movement.[5]

Despite the fact that a large part of Bennett's teaching career was devoted to theology per se, that is not the chief concern of this book. I am concerned, instead, with the way Bennett's theology and social judgments fit together. That the two are to be related has been a constant theme of Bennett's writing; he referred to his first book as a "theological preface to social action";[6] his most recent is *Foreign Policy in Christian Perspective.*

One possible methodological objection to the way this question is investigated in what follows is that the result is an overall "position" for Bennett formed by an amalgamation of data covering a thirty-nine year period. I admit this is a problem. On the other hand, most sections are written to show changes—or lack of them—in Bennett's views. Bennett's most recent statements on an issue are always distinguished from earlier different views. Bennett's writings call for this kind of approach. In the first place, they do not require clarification. They need to be synthesized and condensed. In the second place, they display real continuity not only of substance but of spirit. I daresay that the reader cannot date this quotation:

Freedom is destroyed, objective truth has given place to lies in the interests of state policy, cruelty toward persons . . . has been revived, the peace machinery which seemed to be the one gain from the last war has been sabotaged, and, finally, never far away is the threat of world catastrophe.

Until I tell him that it is from 1936.[7]

[5] Bennett, Editorial: "William Temple" in *Christianity and Crisis,* II, No. 9 (June 1, 1942), p. 2.

[6] *Social Salvation* (New York, 1935), p. xi. He goes on: "This book is a 'preface to action' rather than a program for action but in the end it is the preface which determines the program. What Christians decide to *do* will depend on what they *believe* . . ."

[7] *Christianity—And Our World* (New York, 1936), p. 50.

A project of this nature demands a certain amount of interpretation, and I must confess that I have interpreted the data. I make terms like *perspective, translation, need,* and *welfare* technical terms in a way which is as foreign to Professor Bennett's style as it is, I trust, true to his intention. Perhaps the result forces on his work a schematization that is uncongenial. If that is so, it is an evil by-product of something well meant. What I have tried to do is cut through the humility and irenicism so pervasive in Professor Bennett's writings in order to expose *his* characteristic concerns.[8] If one result is the discovery that his irenicism is virtually a systematic principle, then the inquiry has given us that awareness.

Finally, it remains for me to acknowledge two debts of the greatest relevance. The first of these is to Professor Paul Ramsey of Princeton University who not only encouraged me in the pursuit of this project but willingly engaged me in more candid argument than I can acknowledge. The second is to Professor Bennett himself. Without his help the research would have been much more tedious; one can only wish that the essay which has been the result were done with the grace and clarity appropriate to its subject.

[8] See David Smith, "Welfare and Consensus," unpublished doctoral thesis, Princeton University, 1967, for an extended discussion of Bennett's views on economic and domestic political organization; in the political sphere the present work discusses in detail only his views on foreign policy.

THE ACHIEVEMENT
OF JOHN C. BENNETT

1. THE CHRISTIAN PERSPECTIVE

The fundamental concept in John C. Bennett's thought about religion and society is that of perspective. It is true that this concept is not discussed in all of Professor Bennett's writings. It is also true that many of his more informal statements suggest that his concern lies elsewhere. Nevertheless, from early in his career to the present, it is concern with the establishment of a faithful and true Christian perspective which has dominated his thought. As early as his second major book, *Christian Realism,* Bennett wrote:

Today the task of the Church is to develop among its own people a mind that understands the social implications of Christianity and which seeks to make social decisions intelligently in the light of the Christian social perspective. If we cannot change the mind of the constituency of the Church, we cannot change the mind of the world.[1]

The Church is to concentrate on the establishment of a perspective. If that is not done, anything else it might do would be futile.

The Christian who lives and must act in this world cannot rely on Scriptural legalism, intuitive divine guidance, or on a certainly known policy. Instead, he has recourse to a perspective. Belief in the perspective is no cure-all. Looking at the world from the Christian perspective does not guarantee that

[1] Bennett, *Christian Realism* (New York, 1941), p. 152; hereafter *CR.*

15

one will do the will of God; ". . . but we will make our decisions with a different attitude, from different motives, and with a determination to counteract many of the evils which we foresee as the result of our choices."[2] The perspective is not in itself sufficient, but it is a necessary corrective.

The concept is, again, central in Professor Bennett's most recent book, *Foreign Policy in Christian Perspective.* "In general we may say," Bennett claims, "that Christian faith and ethics offer ultimate perspectives, broad criteria, motives, inspirations, sensitivities, warnings, moral limits rather than directives for policies and decisions."[3] This is in a chapter entitled "The Christian Perspective." The Christian contribution to political discussion begins, although for Professor Bennett it certainly does not end, with the statement of a Christian perspective.

This perspective is made up of certain central theological concepts. For example, in the book just mentioned, it consists of certain affirmations about God, about the command to love, about human nature, grace, and the church.[4] These affirmations are the basis for political and ethical decision making. They can never be ignored by the responsible Christian. This is not to say that decisions can simply be *deduced* from them. They are not absolutely controlling in that sense. In fact, a large part of Professor Bennett's argumentation is designed to show that logical deduction from the perspective is a mistake. But the relationship between the perspective and policy is one question (to be discussed below) and the substance of the perspective itself is another. The first part of this book is devoted to answering this second question: What is the Christian perspective? The discussion proceeds as follows: First, a discussion of the epistemological basis for the perspective, of the

[2] Bennett, "The Christian's Ethical Decision" in *Religion in Life,* IX (Summer, 1940), p. 397.

[3] Bennett, *Foreign Policy in Christian Perspective* (New York, 1966), p. 36; hereafter *FPCP.*

[4] *FPCP,* pp. 35–49.

16

grounds on which it is affirmed. Second, in this and subsequent chapters, a discussion of its substance: what, in fact, one affirms when he affirms the Christian perspective.

Bennett thinks religious decision is an individual matter. The first step in religious discourse is a voluntary affirmation. Religious life, loyalties and insights are essentially voluntary; they cannot be coerced. Yet, once that has been said, it must be added that Professor Bennett has never been content with what some might call irrational or arbitrary decisions as satisfactory basis for one's faith. The deciding person should, he thinks, take two kinds of facts into account. First, and most importantly, he should consider the views of Christians past and present. A Christian perspective is not something one fabricates for himself. It has its source in a specific religious tradition which is not only a given datum from the past, but a living community in the present. Second, and more problematically, his perspective will be influenced by everyday experience. The extent to which it is so influenced, the extent to which there should be non-religious foundations for religious affirmations, is a major problem in Bennett's thought. To get at that question it is appropriate to consider his discussion of the characteristically Christian authorities for the Christian perspective: scripture and tradition.

Bennett begins with the seemingly innocuous assertion that the authorities of scripture and tradition go together. "Scripture includes the earliest tradition," which is to say that it "contains the earliest response of the Christian community to the revelatory events." Scripture includes tradition. On the other hand, the church determined what documents would be scriptural. This choice was made as a consequence of human debate. It was not and is not absolute. The canon remains open in principle. Finally, and most interestingly, the Bible and tradition belong together because the church must constantly reinterpret scripture. Doctrinal or creedal formulas are not absolute. Previous interpretations of scripture remain of interest, although this is more true for the Bennett of the 1950's and '60's than of *Social Salvation*. But those earlier interpretations are suggestive rather than authoritative. The church of the present must read and interpret scripture for itself in the present.[5]

This argumentation suggests that ancient religious authorities are not sufficient unto themselves. Even at the height of the biblical theology movement Bennett never came to the point of thinking that, even within the church, what the Bible says is self-evident. He has had no patience with certain "Barthian" theologians who are narrowly preoccupied with the "internal elaboration of theology," and who thus "lose their critical sense which depends upon the interaction between theological thinking and other disciplines."[6] And, of course, Bennett is even less happy with less subtle absolutizations of scriptural authority.[7]

In other words, in order to make sense of confessional statements one must interpret them using non-confessional ones. Simply to repeat a confessional formula would be obscurantism. Statements of faith must not be isolated from reasonable statements. The relationship between faith and reason, between revealed and non-revealed truth is, therefore, one of continuity, not discontinuity.

Over the years Professor Bennett's views on the relative importance of faith and reason in the determination of religious truth have remained quite constant. In 1933, in one of his earliest and most quoted articles, he wrote that a great strength of theological liberalism was "its assumption of the continuity of the Christian revelation with reason or with natural religion." A "purely arbitrary" revelation having nothing to do with experiences of God "which come to men

[5] Bennett, "A Protestant View of Authority in the Church" in *Theology Digest* (Winter, 1963–64), pp. 214ff.

[6] Bennett, "How My Mind Has Changed" in *The Christian Century*, LXXVI (December 23, 1959), p. 1500.

[7] Cf. Bennett, "Billy Graham at Union" in *The Union Seminary Quarterly Review*, IX, No. 4 (May, 1954), p. 11.

in mere religion or in secular idealism" was unsatisfactory. "Reason," he continued, "can clear away many obstacles to faith. It can build up an argument for the validity of the Christian faith in God which confirms and clarifies experience."[8] Again, as recently as 1966, Bennett has said that although there are no "proofs" of the existence of God, the revelation of God proves its validity in experience. If the Christian revelation is true, "many more of the pieces of our life fit together than if this is not the case."[9]

Moral experience provides the primary confirmation of theism. In this, as in other aspects of his philosophy of religion, Bennett has been much influenced by William Temple. In *Nature, Man and God* the "people's archbishop" argued that the only true obligation was obligation to persons. Thus, ". . . in the performance of duty, especially of difficult duty where the performance is heroic, there is a clear sense of corresponding to, and entering into, a reality which was always there, and which in itself has upon us that kind of claim which can only be exercised by persons." Because this is true, the ethically most sensitive feel that flouting the moral law is "the flouting of what justly claims our reverence." The only justification for this feeling is theism, since *"no Law, apart from a Lawgiver is a proper object of reverence."*[10]

Bennett has argued in a similar vein. "It is when a moral demand cuts across our own desires and interests and runs counter to the approval of our group that we are forced to

---

[8] Bennett, "After Liberalism—What?" in *The Christian Century*, L (November 8, 1933) p. 1404. The kind of argument Bennett had in mind had been formulated by F. R. Tennant in his *Philosophical Theology*, Volume II.

[9] Bennett, "In Defence of God" in *Look*, XXX (April 19, 1966), p. 75. In the same, admittedly popular, article, he has already said that, although there are no "proofs" of God, "there are intimations that the world of our experience is not self-sufficient without Him . . ." (p. 72). In general this article shows how little Bennett's mind has changed over the years. It shows that convictions defended in the past in more technical style have not been forsaken.

[10] William Temple, *Nature, Man and God* (New York, 1934), p. 254.

raise the question: Why is this demand binding on me?" The moral confirmation for theism begins with the fact of obligation to oppose society. "The question here is not, What is the good? but rather, Why should I bother about the good?"[11] For both Temple and Bennett full obligation must be obligation to someone. Given that presupposition there is only one way to explain obligation to oppose the persons in society, namely "to realize that what we choose makes a difference to more than ourselves, to more than society, to God who transcends both."[12] The point is that "the sense of absolute obligation that we sometimes experience" cannot be socially explained.[13] Thus the fact that this kind of experience exists confirms the Christian theistic view. The existence of this kind of experience by itself does not prove that Christianity is true, but it reinforces the conviction with which the Christian perspective is held.

Beyond this, Bennett at one time or another has held that an adequate cosmology must be theistic,[14] that belief in a theistic perspective was psychologically beneficial,[15] and that theism is confirmed by contemporary science.[16]

The details of these arguments need not detain us. Instead we should notice that the very fact that Bennett can attempt these arguments shows that, for him, the Christian perspective must make sense in the forum of reason. In fact, theological assertions should be confirmable by, or at least congruent with, our experience of the world as a whole. When one speaks the language of theology he is not speaking an esoteric language but the most important kind of human language. Theology has a unique body of data, it is true, and Christian theology has

---

[11] Bennett, *Christianity—And Our World* (New York, 1936), pp. 5–6; hereafter *CAOW*.

[12] Bennett, "Christianity and Its Alternatives" in *Christendom,* VI, (1941), p. 360.

[13] Bennett, "In Defence of God" (1966), p. 72.

[14] *CAOW*, p. 5.

[15] See, for example, his article "Are There Tests of Revelation?" in *Theology Today,* XII, No. 1 (April, 1955), pp. 77–78.

[16] *Ibid.,* p. 75.

some unique premises. But those facts do not suggest that the theologian's assertions are not translatable into the coin of ordinary language. They do not suggest discontinuity between religious language and non-religious language. Furthermore, experience which is not obviously religious, for example, moral experience, stands in a very intimate relationship to religious language. In the production of a theological formulation there is "real interaction" between the characteristically religious sources and ordinary experience.[17]

Bennett has engaged in two kinds of argument which tend to support this interpretation of his understanding of religious language. The first of these was a disagreement with Reinhold Niebuhr in the 1930's over the "mythical" element in theology. In *Social Salvation* Bennett claimed that the practice of reviving certain theological concepts, such as that of the fall of man, in the form of "myths" was "the source of endless confusions." Myths may point to objective truths, he admitted, but "the difficulty is that . . . [the myths] also . . . [point] to objective errors. . . ." This is especially likely to happen if the myth is an old and hoary one which many people believe to be literally true. Consequently: "If the theologian who resorts to 'myths' can successfully distinguish between the truth and the error, and if he can successfully explain why he prefers one 'myth' to another, his explanation will probably throw more light than the myth."[18]

In the same year, 1935, Reinhold Niebuhr published *An Interpretation of Christian Ethics,* which begins with an argument for the value of conceiving theological thought as mythical. Myths, he argued, deal with "vertical" aspects of reality which are distinguishable from the "horizontal" aspects with which the scientist is concerned. Therefore,

[17] Bennett, *Christianity and Communism Today* (New York, 1948, 1960, 1962), p. 112; hereafter *CCT*. Although Bennett has thrice revised this book, his revisions consist of additions. When it is relevant the date of a particular passage will be given.
[18] Bennett, *Social Salvation* (New York, 1935) pp. 35f.; hereafter *SS*.

the myth alone is capable of picturing the world as a realm of co- herence and meaning without defying the facts of incoherence. Its world is coherent because all facts in it are related to some central source of meaning; but [it] is not rationally coherent because the myth is not under the abortive necessity of relating all things to each other in terms of immediate rational unity.[19]

John Bennett reviewed this book the following year. Rein- hold Niebuhr, he observed, is "resolved to domesticate the word 'myth' in America." Myths do not represent history in this view but, instead, express essential religious truths. The problem with Niebuhr's use of myths, he went on, is that it is questionable whether, "as a matter of fact, they offer more than illustrations for conclusions to which Niebuhr has come by a rational process." The question of whether or not a myth is true cannot be answered by mythical thinking.[20] Usage of myths for pedagogical purposes was all right, but to suggest that religious language was, in the last analysis, mythical was to remove it too far from the arena of ordinary experience, of the true and the false.

Niebuhr returned to the issue in *Beyond Tragedy* (1937). That which is true in Christianity "can be expressed only in symbols which contain a certain degree of provisional and superficial deception." This is true because the Christian view of the world is revealed and expressed in but not exhausted by the temporal. Thus, "the relation of time and eternity cannot by expressed in simple rational terms. It can be expressed only in symbolic terms." Analogously, artists "are forced to use deceptive symbols when they seek to portray two dimensions of space upon the single dimensions of a flat canvas." In a word, "Every Christian myth . . . expresses both the meaning- fulness and the incompleteness of the temporal world, both the majesty of God and his relation to the world." Then Niebuhr

[19] Reinhold Niebuhr, *An Interpretation of Christian Ethics* (New York, 1935), p. 32.
[20] *The Journal of Religion*, XVI (1936), p. 212.

went on to interpret the Christian doctrines of creation, fall, Incarnation, atonement, and the Second Coming in mythical terms.[21]

Bennett remained unconvinced. Niebuhr seems to believe that the "great myths" are "illustrations of general truth," he wrote, but in fact he holds the general truths "as a result of his analysis of experience and not as a result of accepting the Christian revelation." Thus Niebuhr:

> believes in the Christian revelation because it fits the facts. . . . in his own method he is fundamentally an empiricist rather than a traditionalist, who believes in the insights contained in the myths of theology because they do justice to more stubborn facts than any rationalistic scheme does.

This empiricism was laudable but its covertness and the stress on myth had the unfortunate effect of stimulating traditionalism and credulity in others. Furthermore, the notion that religious language is mythical "gives him an excuse to deal with many intellectual problems in a rather cavalier fashion." This was illustrated by reference to the doctrine of the Incarnation. Obviously, Bennett said, the fall is not historical. Yet what, in Niebuhr's view, is "the relation between the Incarnation and the event in history usually associated with it . . . ? . . . [If] the Incarnation is a historical event, that doctrine leaves us with difficulties which must be dealt with with more precision."[22]

Whether or not Bennett was correct in his assessment of Niebuhr's actual method[23] is a question that cannot be settled

[21] Reinhold Niebuhr, *Beyond Tragedy* (New York, 1937), pp. 3–7.

[22] Bennett, Review of *Beyond Tragedy* in *The Journal of Religion*, XVIII (1938), pp. 336–337.

[23] Robert L. Calhoun also thought that Niebuhr's work was most sympathetically understood as that of an empirical theologian. Cf. *The Journal of Religion*, XXI (1941), pp. 473–480.

For Niebuhr's later views see "Coherence, Incoherence, and Christian Faith" in *The Journal of Religion*, XXXI, No. 3 (July, 1951), pp. 155–168.

here. What one can say is that these reviews show Bennett's instinct for sobriety, his unwillingness to isolate theological discourse. They provide further evidence of his consistent reluctance to separate theological reflection from historical evidence and experience. They confirm the view that his position in the late thirties and early forties was that of an empirical theologian —of sorts.[24]

One must look elsewhere to find evidence of Bennett's continuing allegiance to the notion of the continuity of truth. That evidence can be found in his understanding of the relationship between Christianity and other religious perspectives.

Bennett remains skeptical about whether the mystical Asian faiths can survive in a world which is preoccupied with historical realities.[25] Again, the nationalistic religious loyalties that have flourished in this century can not long endure: "Every friendship between Aryan and Jew, between Negro and Caucasian is irrefutable proof to those who experience it that humanity is one and that racial dogmas are lies."[26] In these cases Bennett's view is that another, this time a non-Christian, form of religious truth will be invalidated by historical experience.

The contemporary faith with which Professor Bennett has been most concerned, however, is Communism. The main thrust of his many discussions of Communism is, of course, that the word *communism* in contemporary usage is dangerously ambiguous since it is associated with a system of political organization, a kind of economic policy, and a foreign policy. One might have different evaluations of it with respect to each of these problems. But Communism also is associated with a religious faith. It is of course not religious in the sense of recognizing dependence on a superhuman spiritual being, but it is religious insofar as it defines man's response to the ultimate, his object of trust for deliverance.

[24] Bennett means, in part, to refer to this stress on the "given" aspects of the world when he calls himself a "realist." Cf. *CR,* p. xi.

[25] Bennett, "Are There Tests of Revelation?" (1955), pp. 81–82.

[26] Bennett, "Christianity and Its Alternatives" (1941), pp. 361–363.

Communism occupies the place in life for the convinced Communist that religions occupy in the lives of their adherents. Communism offers a goal for life . . . faith in redemption from all recognized evils . . . an interpretation of life's meaning . . . [and] the kind of authority that the more authoritarian Churches provide for their members. . . . The Communist like the Christian and the adherent of any of the higher religions is a man of faith.[27]

Thus, "on the deepest level the problem of Communism is a problem of faith and . . . it sets for the Church an evangelistic task of overwhelming urgency."[28] This religious dimension of Communism has certain political consequences; at one time Bennett was quite explicit about this:

. . . Communism as a faith does lead to a totalitarian society which must be resisted by political action. This totalitarian society has behind it the enormous power of the Soviet Union and at times may be extended from country to country by military force. The Church, when it is free to do so, should support the effort to preserve as large an area of the world as possible from Communist domination.[29]

Communism has changed since Bennett wrote those words; his emphasis now is certainly not on the notion that churches should encourage the containment of Communism.

But the fundamental idea the words express, that it is a defect in the Communist faith that lies at the heart of the political problem it causes, has not been given up. The substance of the religious errors of Communism, namely its idolatry and inability to solve the problem of evil, will be taken up later. What is important to notice here is that Professor Bennett thinks of Communism as a faith; that as such it is defective; and that there would be improvement if it were replaced by Christi-

[27] *CCT*, pp. 45–46; see Chapter VII below.

[28] Bennett, "The Responsible Society" in *The Congregational Quarterly,* XXVII (1949), p. 327.

[29] Bennett, "The Church Between East and West," *Christian Faith and Social Action,* ed. John Hutchison (New York, 1953), p. 91

25

anity.[30] It makes sense to him to suggest that Christianity is more nearly true than Communism (considered as a faith).

If Communism is the alternative faith to Christianity with which Bennett has been the most concerned, it is not the alternative faith which he thinks of as the most powerful and dangerous. That faith is secularism. Bennett has defined secularism as ". . . that characteristic of our world according to which life is organized apart from God, as though God did not exist."[31] This faith suggests that the highest objects of devotion are human ideals and causes. It understands man to be simply the product of blind cosmic processes. The roots of secularism lie in our preoccupation with scientific method, in our fragmented and compulsively busy routines of life, and in the anti-religious biases of certain radical social movements.[32]

Bennett is very anxious to distinguish secularism, a faith, from a religiously legitimate and positive attitude toward the secular. The term secular, in this connection, denotes certain areas of human interest and activity which are not and should not be under the guidance of religious authority or theology. Fear of secular*ism* should not force us to deny that the church should allow science, art, and aspects of politics and economics to develop freely. It is all right to have a positive attitude toward the secular.[33]

But secularism is not an adequate religious faith. The Christian response to it should take two forms. First, the Christian should show what phenomena secularism cannot account for (specifically, evil). Second, the Christian must show that his religion can account for these same phenomena. The decision

[30] See, for example, his "The Christian Answer to Communism" in *Theology Today*, VII (1950), pp. 356–357.

[31] *CAOW*, p. 1.

[32] *Ibid.*, pp. 2–4.

[33] Bennett, "Christianity and Secularist Humanism," *Christianity on the March*, ed. H. P. Van Dusen (New York, 1963), p. 129. Cf. Bennet, "The Church and the Secular" in *Christianity and Crisis*, XXVI, No. 22 (Dec. 26, 1966), p. 295, for his criticisms of theologians who confuse the "normative" with the actual secular.

for Christianity and against secularism is a genuine decision, but it is not a "decision in the dark" since the Christian faith illumines large areas of our experience.[34]

In other words, secularism may be partially true but there is another religion, Christianity, which is more comprehensively true. It is questionable whether the secularist's dedication to "compassion for the least of men" can survive without the consciousness that we are objects of divine love, and whether strong but penultimate communal loyalty can be maintained without the recognition that the community is to be judged by God. The values which the secularist cherishes may exist apart from Christianity, but those "which are the chief concern of Secularist Humanism, point beyond themselves to a deeper source of meaning and raise problems which Secularist Humanism cannot solve."[35] It is not so much that secularism is false as that it is less true than Christianity. Christianity, rightly understood, illumines more dimensions of experience.

This is a fairly good statement of Bennett's understanding of the relationship between Christianity and other religions. "There seems to be little doubt," he wrote in an early book, "that of all the great historical religions Christianity is the only one with sufficient vitality to meet the challenge of the new political forms of paganism, to bring the world back to the worship of the God of all humanity who wills for us the community of love."[36] Of course this is said from a Christian point of view. The Christian must agree that there are other approaches to the experience of salvation besides that confessed by Christians. Nevertheless,

It would not be intellectually honest for the Christian to obscure his conviction that, whatever be the saving work of God apart from any conscious relation to Christ, we do have in the Gospel

---

[34] Bennett, "Secularist Humanism" (1963), pp. 139ff.
[35] *Ibid.*, p. 147.
[36] *CR*, p. 161.

the context in which all experiences of salvation can best be understood.[37]

The Christian faith is a confession, but a superior one. It provides Christian and non-Christians with "the surest source of corrections" needed "if the good and the true they share is not to be perverted or at least to become one-sided." The Christian faith is especially helpful with regard to such matters as God, forgiveness, the relationship between the spiritual needs of the soul and the demands of social justice in history."[38]

It must be realized that this is said on a very theoretical level. Bennett is the last man in the world to want to absolutize his own faith, theology, or world view. Furthermore, his discussion of other religions represents only one small aspect of his work; it is by no means the focus of his interest. My only point is to show that, to Bennett, it makes very good sense to ask which of two religions provides the most adequate or illuminating view of the world. The reason this is important is that the only way this question makes sense is on the assumption that there are some, broadly speaking, *experiential* criteria with reference to which "illumination" or "adequacy" can be judged. To say that Christianity handles the problem of evil better than Communism or secularism suggests a yardstick, albeit implicit, which sets standards for adequate and inadequate solutions of the problem.

Thus, as in his rejection of the concept of myth as a designa-

[37] Bennett, "A Theological Conception of Goals for Economic Life," *Goals of Economic Life,* ed. A. Dudley Ward (1953), p. 417.

[38] Bennett, "Christ and the Non-Christian" in *Christianity and Crisis,* XXI, No. 8 (May 15, 1961), pp. 75–76. One wonders how Bennett reacted to the response of Arnold Toynbee: "I have never read so clear and, at the same time, charitable an exposition of what should be the attitude of Christians toward non-Christians. . . ." But, ". . . if a Christian asks non-Christians to accept the claim that certain important truths can be seen best in the context of Christian faith, he will think twice before refusing to make a reciprocal concession to similar claims when these are put forward on the other religions' behalf" ("The Plurality of Religions: Blemish or Blessing" in *Christianity and Crisis,* XXI, No. 16 [October 2, 1961], pp. 163–164).

28

tion for theological language, Bennett's stress on the superiority of the Chrisitan faith suggests his unwillingness to free religious language from the commonly accepted standards of discussion. He claims that once one has become a Christian, one is committed to a world view which is more illuminating than certain other world views.

Bennett denies, of course, that the existence of this greater illuminating power will cause people to become Christians. But what is important is that in principle the unity of truth is maintained. For Bennett religious affirmations evidently have a status like the axioms in a scientific theory. They must be assumed to be true without proof. But they must be confirmed by the data of experience in order to be not only true but valid. On this view certain existential data may suggest a change in fundamental religious perspective. If someone's religion cannot account for certain data, if it is not "confirmed by" them or does not "illuminate" them, then his religious principles are suspect.

Briefly put, while Professor Bennett has never said that a religious perspective could or should be adopted simply on reasonable grounds, he has always maintained that the relative *validity* of a given religious perspective was of the greatest importance. He has always maintained that theology referred to ordinary experience, at least to the extent that a theological assertion must "illumine" that experience. For Professor Bennett theology is a sober, down-to-earth enterprise; as such it can provide the foundation, the premises, for Christian thought and action.

The perspective consists of an anthropology, a doctrine of God, an ecclesiology, and an interpretation of the love commandment.

That the basis for the Christian's action is this broad represents an important change from the Social Gospel period. According to Professor Bennett the social principles of the Social

Gospel were based almost exclusively in Christian ethics, that is, they were relegated to a position of distinctly secondary importance. The result was very superficial social analysis. For Bennett the corrective for this error lies in basing the Christian social message on "the whole range of Christian theology,"—on the doctrines of man and God, as well as on the Christian ethic.[39]

Bennett's views on the doctrine of man represent a good example of the kind of theological work he thinks is important. For, in a sense, what Bennett's writings contain is not so much a full blown constructive doctrine of man as *views on* the doctrine of man as expounded by this or that theologian. Bennett is not interested in a doctrine of man for its own sake. The exegetical or epistemological problems which must be solved before the doctrine can be established do not preoccupy him. Instead Bennett is interested in stating *what* the doctrine of man is, so that one can go on to use it as the basis for loving response to need.

Almost all of Bennett's discussions of anthropology (as of many other matters) take the form of a list of "widely held convictions." This is not to say that they represent the statement of a least common denominator, for Bennett has certainly disagreed with many an "anthropologian." It is to say that Bennett's passion to see the church act for social welfare makes him treat the doctrine of man not as a classic problem to be intellectually explored, but as a basis for action in which we must not lose sight of the forest for the trees. When Professor Bennett discusses the doctrine of man, two questions are in his mind: what can the universal church affirm? and, what

[39] Bennett, "Christianity and Social Salvation" (1938), pp. 6–9. The extent to which Bennett was, on his own terms, a member of the Social Gospel movement when he wrote *Social Salvation* (1935) can be suggested by the fact that that work does not really have a discussion of the doctrine of man. The positive correlate of sin is not the *imago dei*, but salvation. Using Bennett's nomenclature, there is less "theology" in this early work. Of course the nomenclature is questionable since one might hold that *theology* was not discourse about a certain subject, but discourse of a certain kind.

30

consequences do these affirmations have for the church's mission in the world? While these questions never become controlling in the sense that the answer to them is finally authoritative, they are regulative in that they circumscribe the amount of attention that the doctrine can legitimately, even faithfully, command.

The other sense in which Bennett's views on the doctrine of man are representative, is that they show him torn between the liberalism of his predecessors and the orthodoxy or neo-orthodoxy of his own generation. This divided allegiance is clear as early as Bennett's first major article which is significantly entitled, "After Liberalism—What?" Bennett there acknowledged that the most important fact about contemporary theology was the decline of liberalism. The coherent pattern of assumptions and the self-confidence associated with it were vanishing. The premise of liberalism was "faith in man" and the values man cherishes as the clue to the nature of God. Neo-orthodoxy held a very different doctrine of man; other differences followed from this difference.[40]

Given this opposition, Bennett found it awkward to ally himself with either camp. He was sympathetic with the concerns of the liberals, but felt that they needed to be corrected by a more realistic view of human nature such as that suggested by Reinhold Niebuhr in the "much criticized" book *Moral Man and Immoral Society*.[41] The liberals did not take sin seriously enough. Yet, with them, Bennett throughout the 1930's rejected "preoccupation" with original sin.[42] When forced to label himself, he used the word "realist" as a way of suggesting that "the liberal optimism of the past generation and the theologians who deduce their view of human possibilities from a dogma of original sin which goes beyond the evidence are both wrong."[43]

[40] Bennett, "After Liberalism—What?" in *The Christian Century*, L (November 8, 1933), p. 1403.

[41] *Ibid.*, pp. 1404–1405.

[42] Bennett, "A Changed Liberal—But Still a Liberal" in *The Christian Century*, LVI, No. 6 (February 8, 1939) p. 179.

[43] *CR*, p. x.

31

The doctrine of sin was the central topic in the debate about man and his possibilities. From the very beginning of his literary career Bennett has rejected overstressing sin. He rejected an older view of the fall and original sin according to which these doctrines were thought to refer to temporal events which were the cause of the sin and evil in the world. The prevalence of this fundamentalist view at first caused him to completely by-pass the doctrine. "A fall within history does not fit the facts which are known concerning the development of man, and a fall beyond history is an unintelligible idea." Although the idea of the fall may be a legitimate way of emphasizing the fact of evil, "it does create a theological fog." There were other possibilities besides romantic optimism and Augustinian pessimism; one could be realistic about human nature without allowing that realism to harden into a dogma. As Jesus was, we may be realistic about human nature without condemning that nature as such.[44]

Later, primarily under the influence of Emil Brunner, Bennett could affirm the idea of the fall as a non-temporal event.[45] On these terms the idea of the fall represents a "universal truth" about human existence. Men, in fact, everywhere are sinful. But that does not imply that everything that man does is completely sinful. The idea of total depravity does not mean that men are completely depraved; it means that human depravity is of a sort that affects, to one degree or another, the totality of man's being.[46] Too much theological thinking ignores this distinction and begins with an *a priori* judgment not only that everything that men do partakes of the quality of sin but that everything is quantitatively and indistinguishably sinful:

Actually, the fall should be the symbol for the sin that we actually

[44] *SS*, pp. 35–36.
[45] *CR*, pp. 50–51. He refers to Brunner's *Man in Revolt* (Philadelphia, 1947).
[46] See, for instance, *Christians and the State* (New York, 1958), pp. 55f.; hereafter *CS*.

find in experience rather than a doctrine that determines in advance what we shall find.[47]

That men are sinful the theologian may confidently confess; how and to what extent they are sinful is something that must be discovered in fact.

Just what it is one would be trying to discover, what sin in fact is, is a problem his commitment to experience forces on Bennett and one which has been difficult for him to resolve. In his first book Bennett limited *sin*'s referent to "conditions of the soul and . . . definite acts which are the result of deliberate choice." With F. R. Tennant he held that for there to be sin there must be *conscious violation of a standard*. Sin, or "deliberately chosen evil conduct by responsible persons" was distinguishable from other causes of social evil. Making this distinction expedited the solution of those evils because one's definition of the evil influenced his choice of a cure.[48] Both liberalism and neo-orthodoxy ran the risk of oversimplification of the social problem. The one seemed to imply that since everything is sinful there is no reason to strive for any improvement. The other said that since the root of all sin is in the human soul, individual-centered solutions to the social problem were the most trustworthy. Both were inadequate.[49]

The way to avoid dogmatic pessimism which seemed to be associated with the new stress on sin was to stress the fact that social evil has a plurality of causes, "to remain longer than theological discussions usually remain within the area of specific social facts, and to seek to discover the roots of the particular social evils which have driven so many of us to this pessimism concerning the total human situation."[50] This kind of sobriety made it possible to avoid blanket condemnations

[47] *CS*, pp. 53–54.
[48] *SS*, pp. 6–8.
[49] On all this see Bennett, "The Causes of Social Evil" in *Christian Faith and the Common Life* (London, 1938), pp. 195f.
[50] *Ibid.*, p. 176.

which only put people on the defensive. When he sticks to the facts the theologian finds more than sin.[51]

One prominent object of these polemics was Reinhold Niebuhr's doctrine of sin as expressed in his early works, especially *An Interpretation of Christian Ethics.* There Niebuhr defined sin as "rebellion against God." Man's sin, as distinct from his finiteness, "lies in his pretension of being God," but the distinction between sin and finitude seemed finally to be only one of degree. The evil flowing from finitude was like natural evil, Niebuhr held, so long as:

. . . the individual life does not try to make itself the center of existence, but merely makes itself the center of its own existence. Since no discrete and atomic individual life exists anywhere in nature or in human history, such self-centered existence always disturbs the harmony and inter-relatedness of existence. It is, nevertheless, a different order and level from the spiritual evil which is the consequence of trying to make the self the center *of existence.* It is the latter type of evil which is sin in the strictest sense of the word. . . . The distinction between sin and weakness is in the *degree of this pretension* and, not incidentally, as some modern theologians would have it, in the degree of conscious rejection of the good.[52]

Reviewing the book Bennett called for "more light" on the relationship between sin and finitude.[53] Just exactly what the enlightenment should involve was spelled out elsewhere.

First, Bennett acknowledged that Niebuhr distinguished between sin and finitude but claimed that the distinction was not sufficiently stressed. In the passage just cited, for example, it seemed that the weak man was the man who did not have the

[51] *Ibid.,* pp. 195–196.

[52] Niebuhr, *An Interpretation of Christian Ethics,* pp. 81–88. The long quotation is from pp. 87–88 (emphasis added). The example Niebuhr gives of an erring theologian is F. R. Tennant, *The Concept of Sin,* pp. 245ff.

[53] Bennett, Review of *An Interpretation of Christian Ethics* (1936), p. 213.

34

courage to be sinful. Simple self-centeredness was weakness, cosmic self-centeredness was sin. But if the distinction between sin and weakness is only one of quantitative degree, it becomes very hard to attribute certain phenomena (social evils) to sin and others to other causes. This would not be a problem if sin were defined more narrowly as conscious rejection of the good.

Second, the definition proposed by Niebuhr was in a sense too narrow. Surely people do not go around thinking of themselves as God, Bennett thought. That would be very bizarre indeed. Many of the things Niebuhr's view seems to brush off as weakness must be called sinful. To suggest that the reference of the word *sin* be confined to actual rebellion or self-deification "hardly corresponds to the more common sins of complacency and slackness, petty jealousy and all the lesser forms of egoism which make the difference between sensitivity and insensitivity toward the needs of others."

Third, and consequently, Niebuhr's view actually made it impossible to distinguish degrees of sinfulness. Because it was impossible to say which social evils were not caused by sinful acts, we could not discriminate degrees of moral responsibility for social evil. On the other hand, because sin was defined in such an esoteric way, it became irrelevant to an assessment of the various subjective failings with which we are associated. Because sin was insufficiently distinguished from other human frailties it *could* explain everything; because it was essentially too "Promethean" it, *in fact,* explained very little.[54]

These problems were resolved to Bennett's satisfaction with the publication of Niebuhr's great work, *The Nature and Destiny of Man.* There Niebuhr made clear that sin has both religious and moral aspects; these differ from each other not in degree but in dimension:

The religious dimension of sin is man's rebellion against God, his effort to usurp the place of God. The moral dimension of sin is in-

[54] Bennett, "The Contribution of Reinhold Niebuhr" in *Religion in Life,* VI (1937), pp. 281–283.

justice. The ego which falsely makes itself the center of existence in its pride and will-to-power inevitably subordinates other life to its will and thus does injustice to other life.[55]

Furthermore, not all sin is pretension; there is also a sin of weakness: sensuality.

Bennett has never departed far from this conceptualization. When he refers to himself as one of Reinhold Niebuhr's "disciples,"[56] he means to suggest his acceptance of this analysis. For the later Bennett: "Sin is disobedience to God which has its root in human freedom."[57] *Sin* does not describe only those choices for which we have full moral responsibility but includes a wider range. *Sin* does have a necessary moral referent, but our sinfulness has a religious root. We need to be forgiven on a much more basic level than a narrow definition of sin suggests. Our unconscious feelings of guilt and sense of social responsibility demand forgiveness.[58]

Our spiritual neediness expresses itself in attempts to absolutize ourselves. We tend to put ourselves or something which belongs to us in the place of God—not in the sense that we consciously deify that something but insofar as we allow the place in our lives which should be reserved for God to be taken over by our own self-esteem.[59] Thus the very heart of sin is pride, self-centeredness, and the will to power; it is man's failure to recognize his dependence on God.[60] Sin is associated with finitude in the sense that if man were not finite he would not look on the world from a finite perspective; but sin is dis-

[55] Reinhold Niebuhr, *The Nature and Destiny of Man* (New York, 1941), I, p. 179.

[56] See Bennett *et al.*, *The Road to Peace: Christian Approaches to Defence and Disarmament* (Philadelphia, 1966), p. 33.

[57] Bennett, "Christian Conception of Man," *Liberal Theology: An Appraisal*, H. P. Van Dusen and David E. Roberts, eds. (New York, 1942), p. 198.

[58] Bennett, "The Meaning of Redemption in Personal and Social Life Today" in *The Journal of Religious Thought*, III, No. 1 (Autumn–Winter, 1946), p. 55.

[59] *CS*, p. 54.

[60] *CCT* (1948–62), pp. 81–82.

36

tinguishable from finitude because it is its misuse. When finitude is corrupted into self-centeredness, then there is sin.[61]

In all this the dependence on Niebuhr is clear. Yet the old concerns remain. Niebuhr's tendency to stress the sins of the strong man and to ignore the importance of discipline must be corrected.[62] The fact that there are degrees either of salvation or sinfulness must be acknowledged, so as to avoid giving theological warrant to the obliteration of moral distinctions; quantitative assessments of man's sinfulness held on *a priori* grounds are still wrong.[63]

Along these same lines, Bennett has insisted that the doctrine of man includes other affirmatives besides the one that man is sinful. A doctrine of man that only had a pessimistic side would be inadequate; it would fly in the face of the facts.[64] Bennett has always wanted to stress more positive aspects of human existence, but he has never developed the relevant doctrines in detail, perhaps because for him it is enough to know that there is a positive affirmation.

Bennett uses the traditional formula that man was made in the image of God. This affirmation suggests to him that men are rational and responsible beings, that the human soul is restless unless it is devoted to the highest end of human existence, God. The fact that men are made in the image of God, in other words, suggests that they are sinners only by "second nature." It suggests that man himself is of permanent value, that by God's grace men can become new creatures.[65]

Men are not only created in the image of God, they have also been redeemed by God. Warnings about sinfulness are true:

[61] *CCT*, p. 117.

[62] Bennett, "Change and Continuity in the Theological Climate at Union Seminary" in *Union Seminary Quarterly Review*, XVIII, No. 4 (May, 1963), p. 365.

[63] *CS*, p. 55.

[64] Bennett, "The Causes of Social Evil" (1938), p. 196.

[65] Bennett, "The Outlook for Theology" in *Journal of Religion*, XXI, No. 4 (1941), pp. 347–349; cf. "A Theological Conception of Goals for Economic Life" (1953), p. 404.

But such warnings belong neither to the first word about man nor to the last; they belong to what we might call the middle word. The first word about us is that we were made in the image of God. The last word is that "the Word became flesh and dwelt among us, full of grace and truth."[66]

The Incarnation suggests the value of human existence as much if not more than does the notion of *imago dei*. Together these doctrines compose the "positive side"[67] of the Christian teaching about human nature. As such they have two functions.

First, they make clear that human existence, the life of an individual human being is of the highest possible value. If man is made in the image of God and has been redeemed by an incarnation in human nature of God himself, then God has conferred great dignity upon man's estate. The life of a man who is a child of God is the highest social value.

Second, and more explicitly, these affirmations suggest that we can have a kind of sober confidence in men. Bennett once held that they give us "faith in human possibilities."[68] Or, again, "Given that divine grace is generally available, our assessment of the possibilities of objective moral achievement can not be pessimistic."[69] Everything that we have, all our grounds for hope, are in God—that is true. But that is not to say that we have no grounds for hope. It is to suggest that because we have been created and redeemed by God there is no basis for dogmatic pessimism and every reason to have sensible and sensitive hope for social gains.[70]

[66] Bennett, "Toward a Christian Humanism" in *The Christian Century*, LXXIV (March 6, 1957), p. 294.

[67] Bennett, *Foreign Policy in Christian Perspective* (New York, 1966), p. 41; hereafter *FPCP*.

[68] Bennett, "New Emphases in Christian Social Teaching," *The Church Faces the World*, ed. Samuel McCrea Cavert (New York, 1939), pp. 528–529.

[69] *CR*, pp. 51–55.

[70] Bennett, "How My Mind Has Changed" (1959), p. 1500. Thus the real justification for Bennett's "optimism" is the doctrine of God.

This leads to a final preliminary ingredient in Bennett's thought: the doctrine of God. As we might expect, Professor Bennett is, in the last analysis, very unconcerned with God's being in itself. He is concerned with the works of God which we experience. These works may be described under four headings: God is creative; he is righteous; he is involved with history; he saves men.

"When we say that God is the creator we mean that the object of our supreme devotion is one with the reality upon which we depend for existence,"[71] wrote Bennett in 1941. The doctrine of creation does not raise questions of cosmic origins; it is a way of affirming that the word *God* "is not merely another word for the universe,"[72] that God must be differentiated from the historical process.[73] God the creator is transcendent. And, because God transcends the world of the creation one can say that all the creation is relativized. All nations and races have, at least, their dependence on God in common.[74] All political communities and principles of political organization are less than absolute since they are measured by God's judgment and mercy.[75] Social and political life is plastic; it must temper and mould itself to conform to the will of the creator.

Consequently, the affirmation that God is the creator is "the surest way of protecting ourselves from idolatory." While the doctrine does not affirm that God is "wholly unlike" his creatures, it does emphasize God's uniqueness, his independence of everything human.[76] Superficiality on this point is the core of the error of Communism. The Communist absolutizes a particular historical movement and exempts it from transcendent judgment. The movement or party becomes his God. Then

---

[71] *CR*, pp. 22f. The system of capitalization of attributes of God used in the text is the one used by Bennett in *CR*.

[72] *CAOW*, p. 5.

[73] Bennett, "After Liberalism—What?" (1933) p. 1405.

[74] *CR*, pp. 25f.

[75] See, for example, Bennett, *When Christians Make Political Decisions* (New York, 1964), p. 26; hereafter *WCMPD*.

[76] *CR*, pp. 26–27.

when the movement or party becomes corrupted he has no recourse but ultimate despair. Furthermore, absolutization of the cause of the party or movement allows one to sacrifice everything and everyone else to it.[77] This practical idolatory should be much more reprehensible to the Christian concerned with practical welfare than the theoretical atheism of Communist thinkers.

The other side of the doctrine of creation is the affirmation that God utilizes his transcendence in the world; that he is related to the world. The doctrine of creation means that we cannot deny the value of the real world. However, the doctrine of the Incarnation provides another theological basis for the affirmation of the goodness of all existence, and it is easier to find instances of Bennett using this second Christological rationale.[78] The practical equivalence of these concepts is characteristic. What counts for Bennett is the idea that the world is good, that it matters to God. How, on *what* theological basis, this is affirmed, is of secondary importance.

The second major affirmation Professor Bennett makes about God is that he is righteous. This righteousness is not of some esoteric transcendental sort but represents the highest possibility for human beings. This is known to be true because God's righteousness has been revealed in Christ:

The Christian faith that God is known to us supremely in Christ, unless it is accompanied by the rejection of the revelation through the concrete personality of Christ, guarantees the continuity between God's righteousness and the highest human goodness.[79]

If God could take human form, then it must be possible to apply some predicates of men to God and, surely, one of these is righteousness. One could only deny this by making our

[77] *CCT* (1948–62), pp. 81ff. The point is repeated in almost every discussion of Communism.
[78] For example, *CCT* (1948–62), pp. 105–107.
[79] *CR*, pp. 29–30.

moral words "equivocal"; by suggesting that human moral discernment had no theological status.[80]

Thus, although it is true that God's righteousness transcends our righteousness and that we must often question our moral judgments, "when this is done, it should be for the sake of recovering in purer form the highest human perceptions of goodness."[81] We must strive for higher forms of understanding, always confident that "God has a definite character, the character of a Christ-like person." He is loving as Christ is loving. "He is a God of love who deals with persons in ways and within limits predictable because Christian love is predictable."[82] He is, as John Oman wrote, not "circumscribed on every hand by considerations of his own dignity." Instead God is "primarily concerned with our need."[83]

The third major affirmation to be made about God is that he is the Lord of history. History is "the irreversible sequence of events which occur in time and which are the stuff of our human experience." Thus to say that God is the Lord of history is to say: "What happens in history makes a difference to God Himself. . . . He has a will for men in this world, for their public life as well as for their private lives."[84] God is the Lord of the public as well as of the private world. Because God is the Lord of history the Christian who acknowledges him must be publicly as well as privately responsible to him. God's purpose includes righteousness in the corporate as well as the private and personal relationships of men.[85]

In order to understand how God acts in history to make his sovereignty manifest, Bennett can recall his two previous affirmations about God. In the first place, God works in history by

[80] Bennett, "The Outlook for Theology" in *The Journal of Religion,* XXI, No. 4 (October, 1941), p. 346.

[81] *CR,* pp. 27–28.

[82] *SS,* p. 184; cf. pp. 190–191.

[83] Oman, *Grace and Personality* (New York, 1961), p. 41.

[84] *CR,* pp. 30–31.

[85] Bennett, *The Christian as Citizen* (London, 1955), p. 20; hereafter *CC.*

41

arranging history so that eventually good will triumph and evil will be punished. The moral order of the created world makes evil self-defeating in the long run.[86] Bennett often used to quote Berdyaev to the effect that war was making itself impossible; he once said the same of selfishness and an unjust economic system.[67] The idea is that within God's creation ". . . valid moral ideals are descriptions of the demands of reality . . . ; men cannot realize for long that which is opposed to the divine intention."[68] This is not to return to naive optimism. There is no telling how long men "may flounder around in the midst of a divine judgment without realizing in a positive way the intention of God." But:

We cannot organize our common life *permanently* on a basis that is opposed to the intention of God but we can be so weak and blind and sinful that we fail to organize it in accordance with God's intention.[89]

God the creator rules in public life; in the long run good will triumph.

The second major affirmation about God was that he is righteous. That meant that he is moral; specifically that he is Christlike and loving. Correspondingly, the second way that God works in history is through the loving persuasion of men. This persuasion is of three sorts. In the first place, the knowledge that evil cannot succeed induces men to do the good. Secondly, those ideas which are true exert a "constant influence" on the human mind and conscience. Thirdly, God's persuasive power is decisively exerted through "individuals who are controlled by faith and love, through minorities and remnants" such as Jesus and the Old Testament prophets. The leavening

---

[86] *CAOW*, pp. 8–9. The same point is made by Tennant, *Philosophical Theology* (New York, 1930), II, pp. 193–194. For Bennett's detailed discussion of the problem of evil see *CR*, pp. 163f.

[87] Bennett, "After Liberalism—What?" (1933), p. 1405.

[88] *CR*, pp. 33–34.

[89] *CR*, p. 36, emphasis added.

power of courageous human goodness should never be under-estimated.[90]

Not only does the Christian perspective affirm that God is the creator, loving one, and Lord of history. It also affirms that God saves men. The salvation he offers is ". . . a condition in the lives of persons in all their relationships which is directly experienced in this world."[91] Professor Bennett has never given up the idea that salvation could or should be experienced in this world. He still maintains this as late as the early 1950's although with the explicit qualification that final and full salvation is only to be found in a trans-historical realm.[92] We have a taste of salvation here and now, but our full salvation is in the future. It is a goal toward which we are moving.

Thus salvation can be thought of as fulfillment. A saved soul is ". . . on the way now to ever higher and expanding life, to more abundant life."[93] Salvation ". . . should mean the realization in this life of our human possibilities."[94] Salvation is not only redemption from guilt. It is also to be thought of as the realization of our selves as persons. Bennett could agree with John Oman that the God-man relationship is personal in the sense that ". . . its end is to help persons, in freedom and independence, both in their own souls and in the service of their brethren, to fulfill themselves."[95]

The process of being and becoming saved has two dimensions. The first of these is a "joyful trust in the grace of God, a real adjustment of the soul to God."[96] This is blessedness. It is not a static thing but a process. Our consciousness of blessed-

[90] CR, pp. 36–39; cf. SS Chap. VI.
[91] SS, p. 41.
[92] Bennett, "A Theological Conception of Goals for Economic Life" (1953), p. 415.
[93] SS, p. 41.
[94] Bennett, "The Religious Foundations for Social Education and Action," published by the Board of Christian Education of the Presbyterian Church in the U. S. A., 1937, p. 4.
[95] John Oman, Grace and Personality, p. 88.
[96] SS, p. 42, n. 2.

43

ness, of our justification, varies from person to person, and from time to time.[97]

Second, salvation involves goodness or sanctification. This is a "growth towards a perfection which is hardly to be attained in this life."[98] To be saved one must be involved in a process of moral growth. This growth has a personal and a social dimension. Socially, it involves increased concern and responsibility for the welfare of others. Personally, it involves "adequacy-for-life-under-all-circumstances"[99] or the ability to bear hardship and frustration courageously and with a spirit of inner joy.

Both dimensions of the process of salvation may be realized in different degrees.[100] But, in any case, salvation is a process beginning now and culminating beyond history. The saved are those who are on their way to a higher and wider life; the lost are on their way to a starved, narrow and diseased life.[101]

The fact that salvation is understood as the movement of a soul, of a person, toward fulfillment is of the greatest importance in John Bennett's thought and, consequently, of some importance in understanding the kind of writing and work that he has found important. On the one hand, if salvation involves a process of personal growth, then anything which impedes that process is damning and must be opposed. And, of course, there are many things which can interfere with salvation so conceived.

On the other hand, the fact that salvation involves moral growth means that one's salvation forces him to be concerned

[97] Bennett, "The Meaning of Redemption in Personal and Social Life Today" in *The Journal of Religious Thought*, III, No. 1 (Autumn, Winter, 1946), pp. 54–55.

[98] *SS*, p. 42, n. 2.

[99] Bennett, "Meaning of Redemption" (1946), pp. 54–55. Adequacy for life involves being, "personally adequate for the situation in which one finds oneself." The personal dimension of the problem of redemption this concept attempts to describe may not conscientiously be overlooked since ". . . it is a terrible thing for a person to die without experiencing a foretaste of redemption" (pp. 57–59).

[100] *Ibid.*

[101] *SS*, p. 41.

about the world. Thus salvation has social aspects of two kinds. First, through the "influence of social conditions upon the soul" and, second, because "the Christian who is being redeemed must show forth his new life by his devotion to justice and freedom and fellowship."[102]

In other words, social action is both the condition for and the fruit of individual salvation. On the one hand, at the risk of Pelagianism, ". . . human salvation, yes even the grace of God, can be blocked by social and psychological conditions which only human effort can remove." Thus, ". . . human effort, 'good works' . . . must precede the receiving of grace by other souls." And the same conclusion follows from the content of salvation itself:

> The very content of the saved life if it is truly Christian must be activity for social change. . . . The integrity of the Christian depends upon what he does about the injustices which are the other side of his own privileges, and about the conduct of the groups which are controlled by the public opinion of which his opinion is a part.[103]

Early in his career Bennett stressed the difficulties social conditions could erect in the face of salvation. His early works include countless examples of criticisms of people who "oversimplify" the process of salvation. This oversimplification usually took the form of attributing all social evil to sinfulness. Conventional Christians were likely to stress the sacraments, the doctrine of justification by faith, or inner moral change as the key to social reform, to the increased welfare of persons. But, Bennett claimed, this amounted to "a serious neglect of many necessary conditions of salvation—social intelligence, physical and mental health, environmental conditions, changed institutions." In particular, "The spiritual results of unemployment . . . ought to be proof enough that economic conditions

[102] Bennett, "Meaning of Redemption" (1946), p. 60.
[103] SS, pp. 62–65; the quotation is from p. 64.

are basic in the process of salvation."[104] In general, because salvation is experienced here and now (although not in its fulness) it is possible for social conditions to be of a sort that will determine whether a man will taste salvation. As Bennett later put it, "social conditions do not of themselves save souls but they do of themselves damn souls, if damnation is interpreted not as a legal status known to God alone but as a quality of life known to men only too well."[105]

Social conditions are not neutral with respect to the process of salvation. It is undeniably true that people are saved in all different kinds of environments, but that does not suggest that social conditions are irrelevant. Social conditions mould the human personality. "They can even block the grace of God." The fact that some very strong souls have been able to rise above very adverse environments does not imply that environment is unimportant.

. . . only the spiritually developed person can rise above all external circumstances and the world is inhabited chiefly by persons in the early stages of spiritual development. It is not enough for the world to be a gymnasium for saints. It is more important to know whether or not it is a good school and sometimes a hospital for the rest of us. Jesus was interested not primarily in the strong but in the weak and it is the souls of the weak that social conditions warp and break.[106]

As previously noted, however, the only reason for concern with social change is not the fact that such change is necessary in order that others may be saved. Additional motivation comes from the fact that salvation involves moral effort which naturally expresses itself in social action. Salvation is not thought of in terms of "legal status"—if it were, salvation might "not require more effort than the act of baptism."[107] Together, these

[104] Bennett, "Religion: Opiate or Stimulant" in *The World Tomorrow*, XV (June, 1932), pp. 178–179; cf. *SS*, pp. 47–52.
[105] *SS* (1935), p. xi.
[106] *SS*, p. 46.
[107] *SS*, p. 64, n. 12.

two facets of salvation (first, that it is made more accessible by environmental changes, and, second, that it involves dedication to moral growth) provide a strong positive incentive for social action.

There is another aspect of salvation which is also relevant to social involvement and action. That is forgiveness. "To be forgiven," John Oman wrote in *Grace and Personality*, "ought to mean that all need is gone from us to think anything, either in ourselves or in our situation, other than it is. The essence of being justified is emancipation from moral juggling with ourselves by giving us power to look all reality in the face. . . ."[108] John Bennett has always agreed with this. Knowing forgiveness brings the ability to be morally honest, to give up our defensive distortions of our own or our group's worth. Consciousness of forgiveness allows us to be truly repentant for our involvement in evil.[109] The fact that we need no longer be preoccupied with our own goodness means that we can respond more spontaneously to the needs of others.

Thus, in general, for Bennett God is creator, righteous, Lord of history, and redeemer. All these aspects of God's activity are understood to be bulwarks of Christian social concern. God has made the world good; he has revealed what righteousness is; he demands public action toward improvement; he saves men from need for the sake of their neighbors' welfare. What the Christian is to do in response to this activity of God constitutes the remainder of the Christian perspective.

[108] Oman, *Grace and Personality*, p. 209.
[109] Bennett, "The Christian Conception of Man" (1942), pp. 202–203.

2. JESUS AND HIS COMMAND

The Christian perspective involves more than a world view. Bennett has always rejected "the kind of theology which proclaims a Gospel of Grace that obscures the judgement of God and the role of the moral law or of Christian ethics."[1] The Christian perspective includes an imperative. It is the perspective of men who have something that they must do.

Bennett sometimes says that the transition from discussion of what the Christian knows to be true to discussion of what he must do is the transition from Christian *theology* to Christian *ethics*. Whereas Christian theology is characteristically concerned with the doctrines of God and man, Christian ethics is concerned with what God obliges men to do. Then, with this distinction made, Bennett goes on to say that ethics depends upon doctrine, that the imperative is formulated "in the light of the nature of God and man, in the light of what God has done for man's salvation."[2]

From fairly early in his career Bennett has held, against what seemed to him to be the view of the Social Gospel, that the Church's social message must be based on "the whole range of Christian theology" and not worked out simply as an extrapolation of the Christian imperative.[3] At his inauguration as a

[1] Bennett, "Inaugural Address" in *Union Seminary Quarterly Review*, XIX, No. 4 (May 1964), p. 403.

[2] Bennett, "A Theological Conception of Goals for Economic Life" (1953), p. 403, and see above pp. 18f.

[3] Bennett, "New Emphases in Christian Social Teaching" (1939), p. 527.

48

member of the Union Seminary faculty in 1943 he repeated the point;[4] in his book on Communism he notes the inadequacy of the social imperative if isolated from the broad scope of theology.[5] Theology provides the basis for ethics.

Consequently a dicsussion of what the Christian is commanded to do must refer to what the Christian says about God and man, but it must do that in a systematic way. That is to say that the Christian ethic should not be formulated on the basis of one theological doctrine at one time and on the basis of another doctrine at another time. It is possible to avoid this kind of error if one realizes that the Bible has a characteristic center. Jesus Christ provides the basis for a viable Christian ethic as well as for a legitimate Christian theology. He not only reveals what is true but tells us what we should do.

Congruent with his insistence that theology consists of language which makes sense in the historical and public forum, Professor Bennett has always insisted that we have significant historical knowledge of the human person Jesus of Nazareth. While he now acknowledges that theologians cannot "separate the teachings about Christ from the teachings of Jesus,"[6] he does not think that this problem suggests that we know nothing about Jesus. At this point, however, it must be admitted that we are dealing with matters Bennett has not published much about for twenty years or more.

Bennett once argued that the unity in the New Testament suggested the importance of the historical Jesus. The New Testament writers were united, he held, in the conviction that Jesus of Nazareth was important. Paul, for example, "was saturated with what he had learned of the mind and spirit of Jesus, so much so that he could express that mind and spirit without direct quotation."[7] What was important for Paul should be important for us, went the argument. If we give any au-

[4] Bennett, "Inaugural Address" (1943), p. 4.
[5] *CCT* (1948–62), pp. 115–116.
[6] Bennett, "Authority in Christian Social Ethics," unpublished, first of a series of Earl Lectures (1967), p. 6.
[7] *CR*, pp. 127–130.

thority to the New Testament at all we must acknowledge the importance of the Jesus of history.

Specifically, the New Testament writers were concerned with much more than the fact of the crucifixion and resurrection of an individual man. Those events "gain part of their meaning from the context of the life and personality of Jesus. Not any victim could have been made by divine fiat the means of redemption."[8] Therefore any attempt to isolate the cross as a central point of facticity is misguided. The whole narrative of the life of Jesus is important as the context in which the crucifixion makes sense.

Third, not only is the Jesus of history important because he is testified to by the whole New Testament and because his work is inexplicable apart from his life, he is also important as the final source for moral teaching. His teaching is no substitute for theology, but it will not allow us "to escape the ethical demands of God or to forget how central is the love that does not turn away from human need."[9]

Fourth, and more generally, the life of Jesus is important because if we had no record of that life we would have "no norm in testing the many experiences of the contemporary Christ to which men lay claim." A life which is called Christian must have a kind of "continuity with his spirit."[10] The personality of Jesus of Nazareth provides the Christian life with a definite and characteristic norm. Bennett admitted that many "liberal" theologians oversimplified the figures of Jesus and that this led them to call some very bad things Christian. But, he went on, "what limits are there to the use of a vague Christ to justify our purposes?"[11] If we make Christ even more vague than the liberals made him, he suggested, there would be no limits to the extent to which Christ can be prostituted to support an unjust social order.[12]

[8] CR, pp. 131–132; cf. "Inaugural Address" (1964), p. 403.
[9] CR, pp. 131–132.
[10] CR, pp. 132–133.
[11] Bennett, "After Liberalism—What?" (1933), p. 1404.
[12] SS, pp. 92–95.

50

Although he has not subsequently developed the idea, Professor Bennett's notion of what we know about Jesus is very provocative. Very early in his career he claimed that there is "a real unity in the whole gospel portrait of Jesus," a portrait which, its effects suggest, is "an extraordinarily vivid one."[13] Such a vivid portrait was best explained on the grounds that it had basis in historical fact. The New Testament presents us with a portrait of the historical Jesus; like the work of an artist it is interpretative; unlike the work of the photographer it does not appear as undebatable reproduction. But, like the work of a fine artist, the New Testament is faithful to the person of Jesus. For example, we know that Jesus took an attitude toward social outcasts which was definitely different from that typical of his society.[14] It is the portrait of a man humbly, yet absolutely, committed to the succor of his fellow human beings, who gave his life for the welfare of his fellowmen.

In the early 1940's Bennett wrote an article in which he tried to relate his understanding of the Jesus portrayed in the New Testament to other more systematic Christologies.

The trouble with the other views he considered was that they were not sufficiently empirical. An "impersonal humanity theory" seemed to deny the existence of Christ's empirical humanity while a kenosis theory either did the same or did not explain its relationship to the divine. A persuasive modern formulation must begin with the "empirical humanity of Christ." It must acknowledge that Jesus was limited as men are limited, that he had limited knowledge and power.[15] Lim-

[13] Bennett, Review of Henry Frank, *Jesus, A Modern Study,* in *The Christian Century,* XLVIII (February 4, 1931), p. 173. This is one of Bennett's most critical reviews.

[14] *CR,* p. 127.

[15] Bennett, "The Person of Christ" in *Religion in Life,* XII (1943), p. 511. Bennett said that Schleiermacher and Ritschl were the source of his constructive proposal, although he was not satisfied with either of their formulations. Compare von Hügel who insists that being incarnate must mean having a limited human nature and being culturally conditioned (*op. cit.,* pp. 125–126).

ited humanity is the only kind of humanity we have experienced.

On the other hand, a modern Christological formulation need not set itself the kind of problem which the affirmation of the universality of sin caused for the tradition. The notion that sin is universal may be statistically true; it may be true in the sense that all people do in fact sin sometime. But our generalizations about the prevalence of sin must take account of more encouraging phenomena, they "must take account of the human nature of Christ as part of the data, and if they cannot be reconciled with that part of the data so much the worse for the generalizations." The human personality is not essentially sinful and bad:

. . . there is no absolute contrast between humanity and divinity in all respects. Human personality is a fitting medium for the revelation of and the embodiment of essential aspects of God's nature— His personal or moral attributes.[16]

Since human existence can reflect the divine, it makes sense to say that Christ is the supreme revelation of the nature of God. The revelation he brings "comes to us in His personality, in His teaching and in His own religious response to God."[17] Christ is "the surest clue to the nature of God"; his trust in God and commitment to God reveal the form that man's right relationship with God should take.[18] The human Christ reveals what God is like.

Jesus' consciousness was that of a human individual, yet God's revelation is to be found in his human personality. Therefore, "the union between Jesus and God was a union of

[16] *Ibid.;* cf. above, chapter 1.
[17] *Ibid.,* p. 512.
[18] Bennett, *CAOW,* pp. 7–8. Compare Tennant, *Philosophical Theology,* II, pp. 240–241. "Christ revealed God in that he understood Him and has enabled us, not to see *what* he saw without using the same means, but to see *as* he saw by our own 'personally' aided insight and assimilation."

will." The fact that this union took place when and where it did was to be socially explained:

God drew this human will to Himself by the same means by which He draws others to Himself, but the influences which played upon the personality of Jesus—his Hebrew background and the persons and events of his immediate environment—made him fit to be the founder of the new religion which released for all humanity the treasures of the old and made him the center of the whole movement of redemption. . . .[19]

Bennett felt that this theory was not adoptionism, since God both takes the initiative and evokes the response; it was not Arianism since the God revealed is the only supreme God, not some demi-God.[20]

Consequently, "The uniqueness of Christ is as great as we discover it to be as a matter of history." History shows that Jesus reveals what is supremely true, that he is the center of a unique movement of redemption. Others participate in the movement but he is its center. Thus he differs from others in function. No one can take his place at the center of the movement of redemption. The absoluteness of this movement is something which can only be tested by history.[21] We cannot say that either he or it control God's mercy; we can say that without him and the movement which he founded God's mercy would not be real to us.[22]

What then shall we say about the deity of the man Jesus: We can say that in him there was an "act of redemption"; that he was the center of a movement which "far more than any other in history has brought redemption to man." Christ was divine in the sense that God acted in him for redemption. The *form* of God's action upon him was no different from the form of his action on other men. Therefore Christ is to be differ-

---

[19] *CR*, pp. 134–135.
[20] Bennett, "The Person of Christ" (1943), pp. 512–513.
[21] *Ibid.*, p. 513.
[22] Bennett, "The Meaning of Redemption" (1946), p. 55.

entiated from other men in the degree of his "responsiveness" to the divine initiative.[23]

Thus, in terms of this Christology, Jesus' divinity is not a substantive thing. What is divine about him is his will. It is as the man who wills what is good that Jesus is important. He is of the greatest interest as the definer of the good and as an incarnation of the ethical ideal. Bennett's Christology is misunderstood if one does not conclude from it that the ethics taught by Jesus are vital.

And the relevance of what Jesus taught has not vanished with the passage of time. It is undeniable that there have been vast social and cultural changes over the past 2000 years, but these have not affected the permanent and important aspects of human existence; ". . . in the moral and religious life, and even in the stuff of which a good society must be made, the differences between our age and the age of Jesus are superficial."[24] Human nature, its needs and emotions, basically have not changed at all. Since Jesus' teaching must be applied to these basic elements in human nature, its continued relevance is assured.

Bennett's view in early works was that the chief characteristic of Jesus' ethic which must be explained to a modern Christian is its apocalyptic dimension. Jesus thought that the world would soon be brought to a catastrophic end by God. We are convinced that this is not true. Therefore, we must "translate" Jesus' ethic into a non-apocalyptic form.[25] While Jesus was able to act without regard for long-range consequences, we do not have that privilege. Therefore we can not literally take over his ethic.[26] We must say that the ethic of Jesus is "not fully applicable to any age but . . . the regulative ideal for every

23 Bennett, "The Person of Christ" (1943), pp. 512–513.
24 Bennett, "The Relevance of the Ethic of Jesus for Modern Society" in *Religion in Life*, III, No. 1 (1934), pp. 75–77; this is modified slightly in *SS*, pp. 74–75.
25 *Ibid.*, p. 81.
26 *SS*, pp. 78–80.

54

age."[27] The ethic of Jesus is the formal source for subsequent ideals; as such it must be continually re-expressed in material terms.

The basic substance of the ideal proclaimed by Jesus is that human needs, both for spiritual goods and, very importantly, for health and material goods must be met.[28] Jesus was concerned for bodily needs as well as those of the soul, as can be shown by his "interest in food in relation to real need," the petition about daily bread in the Lord's Prayer, the use of bread as a symbol in the sacraments, and his independent attitude toward Sabbath observance.[29] Jesus wanted more than anything else to insure human welfare.

Yet his ethic is not meant primarily as a guide to rules of action or behavior. His primary concern was with human motives, that human beings be motivated by the desire to procure their neighbor's welfare. For Jesus the moral problem was primarily a problem of the "inner life" rather than of overt acts. He wanted to tell men how to be righteous; the way he taught was the way of response to need.[30]

Appropriately enough, then, more than teaching what men ought to do, Jesus embodied the ethical ideal in his own personality. He was not only a teacher about God; he was perfect man. An analysis of his perfection suggests the major substance of the Christian ideal.

In *An Interpretation of Christian Ethics* Reinhold Niebuhr had argued that the ethic Jesus taught and embodied involved a complete repudiation of any form of self-assertion[31] and a complete universalism.[32] This ethic was established vertically, on religious grounds, and not on the grounds that good consequences followed from it. Therefore its unique rigor could not

[27] Bennett, "Relevance of Jesus" (1934), pp. 77–78; this is in *SS*, pp. 76–78.
[28] *Ibid.*, p. 75.
[29] Bennett, "The Religious Foundations" (1937), p. 10.
[30] Bennett, "The Relevance of Jesus" (1934), p. 75; *SS*, pp. 70–71.
[31] Niebuhr, *An Interpretation of Christian Ethics*, pp. 44–51.
[32] *Ibid.*, pp. 52–55.

be explained because of the social circumstances of his time.[33] As we have seen, Bennett could agree with these affirmations insofar as they asserted that Jesus' ethic was apocalyptic, constructed without reference to the consequences. But he thought it unfortunate that Niebuhr seemed to make absolute rejection of the self the very heart of Jesus' ethic. This stress, which Bennett called Niebuhr's perfectionism, set up such a radical ideal that the result of a contrast with the actual could only be pessimism.[34] Not only is such pessimism morally stultifying, Bennett thought, it is unscriptural:

. . . [Niebuhr's] interpretation of love seems to be far too much in terms of feelings which are possible only in intimate relationships and not in terms of a pattern of life which is possible or even desirable in all relationships. He has no clear place for the aggressiveness of Jesus in dealing with evil.[35]

Niebuhr's interpretation of the ideal embodied by Jesus was so radically conceived as to threaten to become socially irrelevant.[36] Bennett could sympathize with Niebuhr's objective in interpreting the command to love as an "impossible possibility," but he was uneasy about the formulation. If the ideal were a little more humane it might be less impossible and more relevant to human life:

Professor Niebuhr seems to me to divert attention from the real center of the difficulty by his extremely perfectionist interpretation of love in terms of complete selflessness and complete nonresistance. His conception of love does not suggest an ideal that has meaning except for the most intimate personal relations. To stress the fact that this kind of love cannot be realized in the world of politics does not point to the most disturbing fact.[37]

[33] *Ibid.*, p. 61.
[34] Bennett, Review of *An Interpretation of Christian Ethics* (1936), pp. 213–214.
[35] Bennett, "The Contribution of Reinhold Niebuhr" (1937), p. 281.
[36] *Ibid.*, pp. 282–283.
[37] *CR*, p. 97; cf. "The Contribution of Reinhold Niebuhr" (1937), pp. 281–282.

The "most disturbing fact" was that human community fell far short of love, so far short as to not even attain justice. With this fact in mind the moralist's view of the ideal with reference to which we contrast ourselves should make clear the whole range of our sins; it should not have the effect of withdrawing attention from frequently occurring kinds of sinfulness.

Niebuhr did not give up his point in *The Nature and Destiny of Man*. There he argued that the perfection of Jesus, the embodiment of the divine ideal, involved an unwillingness to compromise with the relativities of history. The ideal of love, he wrote, is such an exalted thing that:

> . . . there is no self in history or society, no matter how impartial its perspective upon the competitions of life, which can rise to the position of a disinterested participation in these rivalries and competitions. It can symbolize disinterested love only by a refusal to participate in the rivalries.[38]

When divine love is properly understood the freedom and disinterestedness associated with it "can have a counterpart in history only in a life which ends tragically, because it refuses to participate in the claims and counter-claims of historical existence."[39]

For Bennett this approach is overly abstract. It seems to begin with a definition of what the divinely revealed ideal must be and then to interpret the person and teaching of Jesus in the light of that preconception. Who are we to say what forms a human symbolization of the divine may take, he could ask. The fact is that for Christians the divine ideal is represented in the portrait of Jesus. We must extrapolate our ideal from that portrait, instead of drawing a caricature to conform to a theologically appealing conceptualization.

The trouble with Niebuhr's view on theological, rather than methodological, grounds is that it suggests that Christ's per-

---

[38] Niebuhr, *The Nature and Destiny of Man*, II, p. 72. The whole discussion of Christ's perfection is on pp. 70–76.
[39] *Ibid.*

fection depends upon his lack of involvement in social, historical relationships. Therefore, it is "precarious"; it suggests that Christ could only be perfect by being "free from the temptations which accompany the moral responsibilities of most other men."[40] In Bennett's view Christ must be understood first and foremost as a human being. He was not uniquely free from temptation; to suggest that he was would be to deny his humanity. He is not uninvolved; his divinity consists of the fact that he is involved in the warp and woof of history to such an extent that he is the center of the historical movement of redemption.

Niebuhr was right to see that Jesus embodied the ideal of perfect manhood, but his approach was not sufficiently sober and down-to-earth. He did not look long enough at the portrait of Jesus before copying it. If he had looked longer, he might have seen that the image of Jesus presents two ideals, not just one. Jesus is both the perfectly humble man and the perfectly loving man. The Christian must be humble and he must love. These are the imperatives which direct his life. The remainder of this chapter will discuss them in turn.

The concept of humility represents one of the places in Bennett's thought where one wishes very much that his predisposition had been to engage in reflective and systematic analysis. On the one hand, as *Christian Ethics and Social Policy* makes clear, the concept is central to his thought; on the other hand, as a quick look at any of the many summaries of the Christian perspective present in his writings indicates, it is not a concept he has used much. When he summarizes the perspective which the Christian brings to a situation he typically talks about love but not about humility. Sometimes the place of humility is taken by the concept of repentance understood as personal realization of our guilt and sinfulness,[41] but usually

---

[40] Bennett, "Reinhold Niebuhr's Social Ethics," *Reinhold Niebuhr: His Religious, Social and Political Thought*, eds. Charles W. Kegley and Robert W. Bretall (New York, 1956), pp. 66–67; see below.

[41] See, for example, *CR*, p. 82.

repentance is presented as either a precondition for receiving the grace of God, or a dimension of Christian life which in fact has valuable social consequences. In neither of these contexts is the idea of humility elevated to the place of an imperative for the Christian's social life, an imperative which provides a necessary supplement for, if it does not positively parallel, the command to love.

Bennett's first discussion of humility is to be found in the little book *Christianity—And Our World* (1936). There humility was discussed as one of the "Christian graces" along with sensitivity and commitment. Love was said to denote a combination of all three of these things, especially commitment and sensitivity. Humility, in particular, was defined as "the absence of self-righteousness and self-importance . . . having an objective view of oneself . . . seeing oneself in all one's dependence for existence and achievement and welfare upon God."[42] Humility and the other Christian graces were known to be good not on the basis of rational proof but because we appreciate them as good when we see them embodied in persons.[43] Humility then was discussed as praise-worthy in a human character. Its place in the Christian life was analogous to that envisioned for the cardinal virtues in Catholicism.

Shortly thereafter Bennett discussed humility further as it related to the causes of social evil. Here Bennett was concerned with the danger of humility becoming overacute and morbid. It is easy for some of us to imagine the length and breadth of our responsibilities so indiscriminately that we become spiritually worn-out, he argued.[44] When religious humility becomes distorted we should correct it both by analyzing what our actual responsibilities are and by seeking the healing forgiveness of God.[45]

These reflections on the virtues and dangers of humility

[42] *CAOW*, p. 31.
[43] *Ibid.*, pp. 31–32.
[44] Bennett, "The Causes of Social Evil" (1938), p. 179.
[45] *Ibid.*, p. 181.

serve as an introduction to its discussion in *Christian Ethics and Social Policy* (1946). There Bennett says that the love commandment provides the content for the Christian ethical standard, but that "there is also at the center of the Christian life an attitude of humility before God which is a source of ethical guidance." Humility which serves this purpose has three components: awareness of one's personal weakness and sin; measurement of one's self by the command to love; worship of the judging and merciful God.[46]

The command that we be humble is primarily an extrapolation of the ideas that we are sinful and that God is transcendent. These doctrines suggest the infidelity and inadequacy of our willing and acting. They suggest that human social reality will never be beyond criticism. Therefore the individual or groups which would be humble must try to see things from the perspective of another individual or group. The command to be humble is the command to make this imaginative move, to see that our own individual or social interests are causing harm to others. If social groups would be more humble, their relationships would not be characterized by the cycle of self-righteous denunciations which are now all too common. Humility is antithetical to any suggestion that I or my group know what is best for another self or group. It is antithetical to paternalism. Jesus did not lord it over people but gave his life to serve their welfare; we should do the same.[47]

The most important consequence of this stress on humility for Bennett's ethical and social theory is that it gives him systematic justification for not absolutizing a given set of values or social principles. To say that the Christian is commanded to be humble is to say that he is commanded not to presume to tell other people what they must do. He is confined to tentativeness. Thus Bennett's thought contains nothing as definite and general as Reinhold Niebuhr's love-justice dialectic. It is his

[46] Bennett, *Christian Ethics and Social Policy* (New York, 1946), pp. 60–61; hereafter *CESP*.
[47] *CESP*, pp. 65–66.

stress on humility which makes it impossible for Bennett to produce such a formulation.

Bennett is impressed with the great fact of cultural diversity, although, as has been suggested, he believes that one worldview might be more true than others. But he has not been so impressed with this diversity that he will not talk, for instance, about constants in human nature. His judicious unwillingness to pontificate has another root, a religious root, humility. When Bennett refuses to write a social theory relevant to all times and places it is, of course, because he has been made more and more aware of just how diverse times and places can be. But, more than that, he must refuse because a theory which would be Christian must be humble, sober, definitely relevant to the needs of definite people and the welfare of a definite society.[48]

In a word, "If love is the central Christian motive, humility is the major corrective of the distortion of judgment to which all men are prone."[49] In contrast to what seemed to be a danger in Reinhold Niebuhr's reading of the core of Christianity, Jesus' perfection includes his humility. It is the perfection of a man who has certain objectives, to be sure. But it is not a perfection which expresses or demands transcendence of a social location. God, not an ideal, is socially transcendent; Bennett's ideal is the portrait of a social man humble before God.

This stress on humility never means that Bennett forgets that the controlling Christian imperative is the command to love. For Bennett love is not one among many commands, but the comprehensive name for all that is commanded. Or, more precisely, because we are commanded to love we are com-

---

[48] In one of the most responsible reviews Bennett's books have received Roger Hazelton unfortunately argues that Bennett uses humility as a principle more consistently than he uses love. He says that for Bennett love seems to be a name for moral humility. That love is different from humility in Bennett's theory should soon become clear. Cf. *The Christian Century* (November 5, 1947), p. 1334. And see below, chapter 3.

[49] *CESP*, p. 65.

manded to do many other things as well. He could agree with John Oman that ". . . love is no substitute for the moral task, but just a comprehensive name for the full scope of its action and the full height of its motive."[50]

The fact that the Christian is commanded to love may be systematically explained on the basis of two theological affirmations: the fact of God's loving concern for and involvement in the world, and the "positive side" of human nature, the fact that men were created and redeemed by God. Whereas God's transcendence and human sin require humility, his immanence and our exaltation require love. This suggests that love is concerned with something positive, with the possibilities of human existence. Love is not thought of as something which we are driven to do, but as something we are privileged to do. Because God seeks what is good for men the Christian must do likewise; because God has created human beings in his image and redeemed them through an Incarnation, they have an ineradicable goodness which must be realized. The command to undertake this task is the command to love.

If the basis of the command to love lies in certain aspects of the doctrines of God and man, the substance of the command must be understood as the imperative to seek the welfare of one's fellow men. The Christian who is commanded to love is commanded to "seek the welfare of all his neighbors near and far."[52] Love is the name of the command to seek welfare. We are commanded to act so as to make the existence of our fellow human beings more rich, so that their needs will be met. When we seek welfare we seek the end of need.

One can make the command vivid if he puts it in a more personal form: "we should seek for all other persons the same opportunities that we regard as necessary for ourselves and our children."[53] The welfare of all persons, most poignantly necessary in the case of children, is to be our objective. This applies

[50] Oman, *Grace and Personality*, p. 137.
[52] See *FPCP*, p. 37.
[53] Bennett, "The Religious Foundations" (1937), p. 127.

62

to all persons without exception, even if some reasonable calculation forces us to oppose some persons for a time. Love requires that we will "the real welfare of the enemy as persons";[54] it forces us despite our zealous social opposition to their cause to avoid hating them as persons.[55] In contrast to Communism, Christianity requires that we retain a "kind of concern for the opponent as a person."[56] Whereas Communism treats individuals who oppose it as expendable, Christian love requires caring for enemies and for all "marginal people who cannot defend themselves. . . ."[57]

Love which is primarily concerned that human needs be met and human welfare secured will inevitably involve self-sacrifice. But the order of priorities is important. Love is not essentially the effort to be self-sacrificial but the effort to help. Sacrifice is a means to that end. Love is outgoing:

It is sacrificial and willing to pay the price of the cross in the effort to meet the neighbor's need and to realize high possibilities among men.[58]

Self-sacrifice is not so much a command as a description of what will happen if the command is taken seriously. As such it is an inevitable concomitant of a loving life. Someone who is absolutely loving will show that not only in the extensity, the all-inclusiveness of his concern, but in the intensity of his dedication. Love "demands singleness of mind. It must forgive seventy times seven. It must be willing to pay the price of the Cross."[59] On the subjective side love involves "completeness of self-giving"[60] or total unconcern for self.

[54] Bennett, "The Hardest Problem for Christian Ethics," *Christianity and the Contemporary Scene,* eds. Randolph Crump Miller and Henry H. Shires (New York, 1943), p. 127.

[55] *Ibid.,* p. 126.

[56] *CCT* (1948–62), p. 96.

[57] *WCMPD,* p. 29.

[58] Bennett, "The Christian Bases for Enduring Peace," *Approaches to World Peace,* eds. Lyman Bryson *et al.* (New York, 1944), pp. 747–748.

[59] Bennett, "Relevance of Jesus" (1934), p. 75; *SS,* p. 71.

[60] *CESP,* p. 15.

Love, understood in this way, is the standard that should rule our motivations. All decisions, whether affecting the private sphere of personal and family practice or the national political ethos, should be made with the welfare of all those affected in mind.[61] Love, rather than faith or hope, is to be the primary motivation for Christian action.[62]

No matter how ambiguous our deeds may be, our motives should always be in conformity with love. One should always want to secure welfare and should be moved to act with that in mind. Thus our attitude toward the decisions we make will be one of concern for the effects those decisions may have. If these effects harm individual persons, we should never allow it to be said that we meant that harm to occur. That it does occur will suggest discontent with the alternatives available to us and cause us to work so that other choices will be available in future situations.[63] Christians are people who care; they are sensitive. Guided by love, they "should form a minority which really care about the effects of national policy. . . ."[64]

Of course it is true that no one is ever fully loving, that no one lives up to this ideal. But that does not mean that we can exclude some of our willing from the jurisdiction of the love commandment.[65] No boundaries can be drawn to suggest its range of application, no degree of commitment labeled ahead of time as impossible for it. The Christian is obliged in his most fundamental desires to seek the welfare of his fellow men.[66]

The stress on love as the standard for motivation is important because motives are important. They are the stuff of

[61] *CESP,* p. 61.
[62] Bennett, "What May We Hope for in Society?" in *Congregational Quarterly,* XXI (1953), p. 113.
[63] Bennett, "The Outlook for Theology" (1941), pp. 350–351.
[64] Bennett, "The Christian Bases for Enduring Peace" (1944), p. 748.
[65] Bennett, "The Hardest Problem for Christian Ethics" (1943), pp. 124–125.
[66] Bennett, "Christian Ethics in Economic Life," *Christian Values and Economic Life,* eds. John C. Bennett *et al.* (New York, 1954) pp. 205–206.

64

character. Furthermore, it is historically true that one's motivations affect his actions. If we know that a man is motivated in such and such a way, we can predict that he will tend to act in a correlated kind of way. Constancy of motivation tends to mean constancy or dependability of action. Finally, a given action is not an isolated entity, but occurs in a personal context. Consequently the motives which prompt it are important because they affect the consequences of the act.[67] The effect of giving a student a bad grade on a paper, for example, will depend on the motive from which it was done. If the student feels it was done from malice the result will be wrath; if he feels it was done because the professor thought that more was within this student's reach, the result may be better work in the future.

Yet, as this kind of utilitarian justification of concern for motivation suggests, love must be thought of as more than a criterion for motivation. Motivation can never be separated from consequences. Love must measure our actions and should keep our pattern of activity under "relentless criticism." Actions that harm persons should be acknowledged for what they are. When we measure our actions by love we see that we must avoid "deceiving ourselves concerning the evil in our choice by a verbal trick, which changes the . . . [evil's] character by identifying it with our duty. . . ."[68]

This is not to say that on the basis of an understanding of love we can produce a detailed set of rules or definitions which describe certain things that are always right or wrong. It *is* to say that we are always commanded to seek human welfare, and that that means we should always be concerned with the adverse consequences of our actions, however necessary the action may be. It is to say that love "intends the best available combination of consequences for all neighbors" rather than that love involves ingrown concern with "the avoidance of

[67] Bennett, "The Hardest Problem for Christian Ethics" (1943), p. 125.

[68] *Ibid.*, pp. 125–126.

65

particular acts that are absolutely condemned in advance by a law whose full applications are not known."[69]

As this kind of comprehensive guide to Christian action, love serves as a kind of principle of criticism for institutions, proposals for social change, and methods of bringing that change about. Concern for the needy means concern for the society in which he lives. When we seek the real welfare of others we are driven to "oppose those social conditions which obstruct and destroy that welfare," to seek to reform social institutions which "crush persons."[70] Moreover, the Christian must be concerned with social justice and mutuality in social groups because the realization of these values makes it easier for individual Christians to lead lives of love.[71] There is a sense in which it is easier to be a good Christian in a good society than in a bad one; the good society will not allow so many of one's choices to have bad consequences.

Both because social injustice means the impossibility of the welfare of others and because it inhibits our own spiritual growth, we must will "a structure of social justice as the condition for all forms of life that are on a higher level than justice."[72] Love for the neighbor must include "the struggle for a social order that is favorable to the real welfare of all neighbors."[73] Love requires us to seek social welfare.

But what social welfare involves has to be defined. The definition will not be a set of "thou shalt not's." Instead it will be an articulation of the standards and goals which the welfare of human beings requires; goals such as justice, fellowship, the protection of the individual, and so forth.[74] Love wills these

[69] Bennett, "Protestant Ethics and Population Control" in *Daedalus*, LXXXVIII, No. 3 (1959), p. 455.

[70] Bennett, "Religion: Opiate or Stimulant" (1932), p. 179. Recognition that this was necessary was the permanent gain in the Social Gospel movement according to Bennett.

[71] Bennett, "The Relevance of Jesus (1934), pp. 79–80.

[72] *CR*, pp. 78–79.

[73] *CCT* (1948–62), pp. 107–108.

[74] Bennett, "The Christian's Ethical Decision" (1940), pp. 397–398. Much of this article is incorporated in *CR*.

principles as a means to an end, the end of human welfare.

Bennett's form of making this transition from the Christian imperative of love to generally acknowledged social values such as justice (which will be discussed further in the following chapter) is distinguishable from that of his friend and colleague Reinhold Niebuhr. Granting that Niebuhr often changed his mind on this issue and that this book can not hope to adequately represent his position, one can say that there is a definitely idealistic color to his discussion. In the early, and since repudiated, book *An Interpretation of Christian Ethics*, Niebuhr had this to say about the relationship between love and justice:

The ideal of love and the ideal of equality . . . stand in an ascending scale of transcendence to the facts of existence. The ideal of equality is a part of the natural law which transcends existence, but is more immediately relevant to social and economic problems because it is an ideal law. . . . The ideal of love . . . transcends all law.

Equality is "a rational, political version of the law of love"; it is the fundamental principle of justice. In a word:

As the ideal of love must relate itself to the problems of a world in which its perfect realization is not possible, the most logical modification and application of the ideal in a world in which life is in conflict with life is the principle of equality.[75]

Since one cannot have love in the historical world characterized by sin and finitude, Niebuhr seems to say, let us have the next best thing: equality and justice. It would be good if we could

[75] Niebuhr, *An Interpretation of Christian Ethics*, p. 136. For an example of another side of Niebuhr's thought see his concluding essay in the Kegley and Bretall volume previously cited. Niebuhr is describing his early views: "I tried to make the transcendence of love over law to mean the indeterminacy of love as against the determinate obligations which are defined in natural law" (p. 434). Insofar as that is all that Niebuhr has meant by transcendence he and Bennett have been in agreement.

have love, but *in principle* we cannot so let us settle for the next best thing. Equality is to be desired by the Christian because it is the closest possible approximation to love.

This motif is still present in *The Nature and Destiny of Man*. There Niebuhr says that the relation of mutual love to principles and rules of justice is "positive" insofar as the rules and principles are rationally (or, generally) conceived.[76] The relationship is "negative" insofar as, and because, all systems of principles and rules are sinful and express the interests of certain particular groups. Among these social principles, however, equality is still the closest approximation to love:

Equality as a pinnacle of the ideal of justice implicitly points towards love as the final norm of justice; for equal justice is the approximation of brotherhood under the conditions of sin.[77]

Again, earlier in the same work:

Love is . . . the end term of any system of morals. It is the moral requirement in which all schemes of justice are fulfilled and negated. They are fulfilled because the obligation of life to life is more fully met in love than is possible in any scheme of equity and justice. They are negated because love makes an end of the nicely calculated less and more of structures of justice.[78]

Since we cannot have the higher, better, ideal we must make do with its vicar, with the least adulteration the conditions of political reality will allow.

For Bennett, as I have suggested, love is not such a radically unattainable ideal. It is "a real caring for the welfare and dignity of all our neighbors, even those whom we never see. . . . " This kind of love will be forced to will "justice for others" not because justice is the next best thing possible but because a just social life is "essential to the welfare of people every-

[76] Niebuhr, *The Nature and Destiny of Man*, II, pp. 248–249.
[77] *Ibid.*, p. 254.
[78] *Ibid.*, I, p. 295.

68

where."[79] The relationship between love and justice is not fundamentally that between the perfect ideal and its closest possible approximation; it is the relationship between whole and part, between end and means. Social principles are not logical approximations of love; they are means to the end of love.

The crucial concept for understanding Bennett's view is the concept of welfare. For Bennett, love wills everything that will be for someone's welfare. That means that love wills many things for people. The Christian does not simply will some esoteric religious good for men, but:

He will be guided by the claims of many forms of human good which have their proper place and which become dangerous only when they . . . become, in isolation, the chief objects of devotion.[80]

Christian love involves "the serving of many values which contribute to the welfare of the neighbor." This means that values such as freedom and justice are Christian in the sense that ". . . Christians from the motive of love, must seek whatever values are essential for the welfare of persons."[81] Other values are not inferior approximations of love; they are the very stuff of human welfare. Love must be *translated*[82] into the language of these social values, that is, it must articulate a perception of human need in terms of them.

Thus the concept of love is both the summation and the end of the Christian perspective. It is the summation since, along with humility, it represents the explicit ethical formulations of a world view oriented through and through toward action to insure the welfare of human beings. On the other hand, the command to love is the end of the Christian perspective since

[79] Bennett, "Reinhold Niebuhr's Social Ethics" (1956), pp. 57–58.

[80] Bennett, "A Theological Conception of Goals for Economic Life" (1953), p. 420.

[81] *Ibid.*, p. 421.

[82] Bennett, "Christian Ethics and Current Issues," a pamphlet containing the M. T. Burt Lectures at the Cotner School of Religion, (Lincoln, Nebraska), p. 13.

it requires that the Christian work for social welfare. Welfare, then, is defined not in religious but in political terms. It involves social justice and freedom (these principles will be discussed below). Thus in order to move from the perspective to social action, one must perceive what is essential to human welfare. We must now consider further dimensions of this process of perception and translation.

3. TRANSLATION AND NATURAL LAW

Fundamentally the Church's social task consists of defense of the Christian perspective. If that is done successfully the necessary social action will tend to follow. But the perspective not only motivates; it also directs action. This is an idea which Bennett has defended as recently as 1967. The way in which it is affirmed represents one of his most refined, if controversial, theological formulations. He writes:

> We can never predict when theological thinking may be the source of guidance for social decision or perhaps the source of inhibition against a particular type of social action. . . . Nevertheless we cannot expect to deduce social policy from theology. It is likely to be a stimulus and a corrective that leaves many ethical questions open that have to be answered on grounds that are essentially non-theological. But it takes theology to criticize theology.[1]

Theology, the perspective, is a source of guidance, but it is not an all-sufficient source. How and why does theology serve as a source of social guidance and correction?

As was shown at the conclusion of chapter 2, Bennett does not understand the relationship between love and social principles, such as justice, as the relationship between something transcendent and something human. Insofar as he has a consistent position on this issue, his view is not so much that justice is a lesser approximation of love as that justice is a different kind of thing from love. He does sometimes refer to

---

[1] Bennett, "Authority in Christian Social Ethics" (1967), pp. 3–4.

71

the "transcendence" of the Christian ethic but such a reference should suggest, in the first place, not the unattainableness but the inescapableness of that ethic for the Christian.

Yet other general principles besides the Christian perspective are necessary for a Christian social ethic. Bennett can even suggest that they correct the Christian ethic. Affirmation of the principle of justice keeps those who think that love is enough from misusing their power over others.[2] It counteracts paternalism. Moreover, broad social criteria are related to love in an odd way. As "ways of spelling out what the good of the neighbor is in the world as we know it," they "cannot be derived from Christian love alone but from Christian love as it seeks knowledge concerning the needs of the community of neighbors."[3]

This does not mean that love does not have a controlling affect on the social values the Christian should defend. It means that those values cannot be *deduced* from love. The relationship between love and such a value as justice is not one of deduction, but one of translation. For Bennett the first step in the formation of a Christian social ethic is the translation of the language of faith into the language of politics. "Christian love in the heart of citizens can be translated into terms of such generally recognized values as justice and order and peace and freedom."[4] In what follows we will discuss what is involved in this process of translation.

In general, the ability to translate presupposes a common referent of the words involved. I only know that the English word *horse* and the German *das Pferd* are two ways of saying the same thing because I know that they have a referent in common. There is a third thing, the perception of (a) horse

[2] Bennett, "The Demand for Freedom and Justice in the Contemporary World Revolution," *Religion and Culture,* ed. Walter Leibrecht (New York, 1959), p. 325.

[3] Bennett, "Principles and the Context," Unpublished Presidential Address to the American Society of Christian Ethics (1961), pp. 11–12. Cf. *Worldview,* V, No. 2 (February, 1962), pp. 3–7.

[4] *FPCP,* pp. 37–38.

which enables me to equate them. Similarly, for Bennett, there is a perception that relates the concepts of love on the one hand, and broad criteria such as justice on the other. It is the perception of the needs of human welfare.

Naturally, what people need changes from time to time and from place to place. Thus there are no universal and necessary formulations of the translation of the language of faith into the language of politics. Bennett means to do justice to this fact when he repudiates "deductive ethical rationalism,"[5] or when he asserts that there is no universal principle for relating such social values as order, justice, and freedom."[6] The "exact pattern" of the relationship of these values depends upon "the special needs of each situation."[7] The application of general moral principles to particular situations cannot be certainly determined in advance.[8] Protestants, in particular, "cannot find a Christian law which determines in advance how we should relate . . . principles such as justice and freedom to each other." In fact they may find that these principles conflict with each other.[9] Noting some support for his position in Reinhold Niebuhr's thought,[10] Bennett insists that just as human needs change, so the priorities among broad criteria must change.

On the other hand, what human welfare requires, what is needed, retains some constancy. This suggests Bennett's disagreement with those theological moralists he calls "contextualists" who seem to him to ignore important ethical problems.

[5] Bennett, "Principles and the Context" (1961), p. 7.
[6] Bennett, "Goals for Economic Life" (1953), p. 422.
[7] Bennett, "Freedom and Justice" (1959), p. 333.
[8] *CESP,* p. 122.
[9] Bennett, Review of Edward Duff, S.J., *The Social Thought of the World Council of Churches,* in *Religion in Life,* XXVI (1957), p. 305.
[10] Bennett, "Reinhold Niebuhr's Contribution to Christian Social Ethics," *Reinhold Niebuhr: A Prophetic Voice in Our Time,* ed. Harold R. Landon (Greenwich, Connecticut, 1962), pp. 74–75. He attributes to Niebuhr a "relativism of the concrete decision" which "is really the effect of relating to each other . . . permanent criteria and of relating all of them to the contingent and quite unpredictable circumstances which call for action." Of course, this is a good characterization of Bennett's own view.

Specifically, they ignore the need for criteria for making social decisions. They seem to blur the distinction between "ethical guidance that is relevant to policy" and "the sources of morale, of attitudes which make policy more tolerable as we seek to implement it."[11] In their admirable stress on the value of spontaneity of motivation, they suggest that one can do without social criteria.

Yet, according to Bennett, they themselves make use of such criteria, as any reading of their works will show. "The most absolute contextualist is sure to make use of bootlegged principles," Bennett wrote in 1961—and then went on to show the use of such principles by Barth and Bonhoeffer.[12] With reference to Paul Lehmann and Richard Shaull he argues that such concepts as humanization and *koinonia* really serve as the equivalent of social criteria formulated in terms of principles.[13] Since the use of social criteria is unavoidable, one's theory should take that fact into consideration; an ethic of inspiration has some value but it "cannot be self-sufficient."[14]

Given that there must be broad social criteria, Bennett's fundamental disagreement with a "contextualist" could be described as a debate over the range or extent of the context. He insists that decisions about social criteria (which, for him, are made with reference to the securing of human welfare) must refer to a context wider in space and time than the moment of decision. Temporally:

We must do much thinking in advance about the relation between these criteria or objectives, about their interdependence, even if such thinking cannot produce for us a law. For example, it is important to have some clear ideas about how we arrange order and freedom in terms of priority.

[11] Bennett, "Principles and the Context" (1961), pp. 9–10.
[12] *Ibid.*, pp. 1–5.
[13] Bennett, "Epilogue," *Christian Social Ethics in a Changing World,* ed. John C. Bennett (New York, 1966), pp. 375–376.
[14] Bennett, Review of *The Social Thought of the World Council of Churches* (1957), p. 304.

The arrangement of the criteria cannot be absolutely frozen in advance, but it is important that "advance thinking" be done.[15]

The context must be widened so as to include the judgments of those who look on the situation from a different perspective. If we put all our emphasis upon the situation, "we may be determined too much by the limitations that it places upon our vision."[16] This suggests the value of the church as a forum for social debate. Broad imperatives should be known within the church, not just "as some individual Christian citizen mixes them with the stuff of politics."[17]

The root error of a contextualist ethic, thus, is that it provides "no protection against one's being captured by the situation where it is experienced with great intensity."[18] The contextualists' rejection of *universal* principles is not so intolerable; to accommodate them Bennett is willing to make use of the phrase "moral pressures" to describe the elements that must be brought to the situation.[19] He freely admits that the decision among various principles must be made on the spot, but he insists that such a decision must be understood to be a choice among various "moral values and goals and principles which all have a claim upon us but which are in some measure of tension with each other. . . ."[20] Hard decisions should be made "because of goals which are defensible on the basis of some principles and we should know in the light of what principles the decisions are hard."[21]

Bennett grants that the Christian individual must take the responsibility for his own decision as he confronts a given set of circumstances. Yet:

[15] Bennett, "Principles and the Context" (1961), p. 11.

[16] *Ibid.*, pp. 19–20.

[17] Bennett, "Authority in Christian Social Ethics" (1967), pp. 10–11; and see chapter 4.

[18] *FPCP*, p. 38.

[19] *FPCP*, p. 39; "moral pressures" is also used in the reference at n. 18.

[20] *WCMPD*, pp. 102–103.

[21] Bennett, "Principles and the Context" (1961), pp. 8–9.

. . . what actually takes place is a narrowing of the morally defensible alternatives. There are boundaries within which action takes place which can be discerned in the light of what we bring to the concrete situation. We do not enter that situation blind or equipped only with a commitment to find the will of God in it, . . . we need to know as much as we can about the price we pay in terms of one objective as we seek to do justice to another.[22]

As was argued above, Bennett does not want to set up a number of prior definitions of acts which will always be right or wrong. He does claim that human social existence is complicated to the point that there are times when what one must do will have adverse consequences. He thinks it is important that one realize the complexity of the field in which he acts, because if he fails in this he is likely to do more harm than good.

One way to make his point clear is to examine a criticism which has been made of it. In *Situation Ethics* Joseph Fletcher quotes the thematic sentence from Bennett's essay of 1943, "The Hardest Problem of Christian Ethics": "There are situations in which the best that we can do is evil."[23] Fletcher then goes on to dissociate himself from this view which he seems to characterize as an "intrinsicalist" one. Fletcher claims that if one does the loving thing it cannot also be evil. He uses as an example the case of a small merchant who must lie to divert some racketeers from their "protection" victim. He says that

---

[22] *Ibid.*, p. 18.

[23] Joseph Fletcher, *Situation Ethics* (Philadelphia, 1966), p. 64. The quotation from Bennett is found on p. 119 of his essay. Bennett always refers to Emil Brunner in this connection. Brunner wrote that the perception of the distinction between what God wills (love) and what we must do (orders of creation) only leads to repentance when one realizes that the distinction cannot be avoided. The depth of original sin and evil are not seen, he held, "until we are *obliged* to do something which in itself is evil, that is, we do not see this clearly until we are *obliged* to do something in our official capacity—for the sake of order, and therefore for the sake of love—which, apart from our 'office' would be absolutely wrong" (*The Divine Imperative* [Philadelphia, 1947], p. 227; emphasis in original).

a view like Bennett's must hold that the merchant did an evil act, whereas for his "situation ethic" that is not true.

In contrast, as was brought out before, Bennett insists that the moral necessity of an act should not blind us to its immoral dimensions. A man is not often confronted with the alternative of choosing either this option for the sake of life or that one for the sake of his own self-satisfaction (which is the alternative facing Fletcher's merchant). More typically, one must opt for one life or another, for the happiness of this man or the security of that child. Bennett claims that one is irresponsible if he is not articulate about the criteria in terms of which he will make these decisions and dishonest if he does not admit that he must sometimes compromise one principle for the sake of another.

Bennett's theoretical way of accounting for the ambiguous character of any social choice is to say that when love is translated into political language its correlate is not one particular value or principle which serves to decide all cases, but a complex of principles arranged in varying patterns.[24] Just how they are to be arranged will be determined by the needs of welfare. Take a counter-example to Fletcher's case. Suppose that a school bus driver finds that his brakes fail on a slippery hill. He must either allow his bus fully loaded with children to plummet over an embankment or steer it so that it will be stopped by a cliff on the other side of the road. Directly in his path on the latter course are two small children. For Fletcher this does not properly speaking pose a moral dilemma; the driver can run down the two youngsters and not have done something evil. For Bennett the same choice would follow, but there would be no self-confident assertion that what one had done was unequivocally loving.

More characteristic of Bennett is the use of an illustration from foreign policy. Suppose a government faces the alternative of either taking up arms or allowing a neighboring state to be

[24] Compare Fletcher: "Love and Justice are the Same," *Situation Ethics,* Chapter V.

overrun by aggressors. On Fletcher's terms it might, depending on the circumstances, choose whichever of these alternatives had the best consequences. This choice would not be evil because it would be the most loving thing that could be done in the situation.

Bennett would not find the matter so simple. He could say that the consequences facing the people invaded are complex. They might involve increased material prosperity with a decrease of freedom. This decrease in freedom might go hand in hand with either a higher or lower level of justice. Conquest might make the society more or less egalitarian. As one tried to decide what was the loving thing to do for these people, his first step would be to ask what it was they needed.

Suppose he came to the conclusion that they needed the imposition of a social regime which would provide them with food. With this in mind he would allow the conquest to take place. But he would admit that the people needed some things besides bread—for instance, that they needed freedom. He would also remember that there had been just men in the society who had worked for reform and that many of these men would be killed by the invaders. He would be concerned for the welfare of such men. In short, he would acknowledge that while his decision was the most justifiable one possible, it had evil consequences for which he was responsible. He would not be so perfectionistic as to feel compelled to deny that "there are situations in which the best that we can do is evil."

It is the fact that love and other social criteria are joined by reference to welfare that enables Bennett to reason this way. On Fletcher's terms the evaluation of an act must make use of one of two predicates: loving or evil. Since love and evil exhaust the possibilities, an act must always be either loving or evil. Obviously, in this framework, Fletcher can never say that one should do the evil *instead of* the loving thing. For Bennett love is opposed to evil, of course, but, more precisely, it wills that people's needs be met and that their welfare be assured. The evils from which men *need* to be delivered are manifold;

evil is as diverse as need. Consequently, the possibility remains open that in securing one kind of welfare one will only enhance human neediness in another sphere. Almost invariably we must make a choice among kinds of need. Therefore we must very frequently do something that is evil. On the question of the priorities among kinds of need Bennett is systematically undogmatic; he is constantly critical of those who imply that need and welfare are obvious and unequivocal matters.[25]

Thus, love's demand must be articulated in terms of frequently divergent social values. But how is one to decide which articulation, which set of values, is most adequate to a particular time and place? How should one go about discovering the best way of translating love into social criteria? If one does not "deduce," to what standards does he appeal? Should he appeal to faith? Or, to experience?

In a very early article Bennett suggested that there were two tests for legitimacy which should be applied to social principles. The first of these was, broadly speaking, utilitarian. One should defend those ways of life which do not lead to "blind alleys of stagnation or collective suicide," that is, "We must test ethical conduct by its consequences in terms of a minimum conception of welfare." Yet this utilitarian test was not sufficient. It needed to be supplemented by "moral intuition." This meant "We must consider our attitude toward a way of life when we see it embodied in persons." Altogether:

[25] On all this see Bennett's review of Fletcher, *Situation Ethics* in *Religious Education,* LXI, No. 6 (November–December, 1966), pp. 482–483. Bennett argues that Fletcher understands love incorrectly: "Since love seeks the welfare of all neighbors affected by what we do or leave undone, ethics must have more to say about what constitutes that welfare" (p. 482). Furthermore, there may be "tension" between the ingredients of welfare: ". . . usually when we subordinate an important principle that guides conduct to some other consideration, that principle should still help to correct what we do and should not be 'set aside' " (p. 483). Bennett uses torture as an example of a kind of thing that is always (he says "intrinsically" and "inherently") against human welfare.

79

We can have most confidence in the result when there is mutual support for our moral judgments from the nature of the consequences which follow upon our conduct and from the judgments of value which are widespread enough to be truly representative of most types of humanity.[26]

With this in mind there was no basis for moral skepticism. "Moral landmarks" for personal and social life could be found which are "so deeply grounded in the structure of life that it is not too much to claim for them permanent and universal validity."[27] Bennett then proceeded to repudiate individual and collective egoism and to argue for democracy, personal discipline, and integrity on these grounds. Love, a characteristically religious criterion, was not mentioned.[28]

The confidence in general human reason and goodness this and other early statements reflect was not deserted when Bennett came back to the problem in 1946 in *Christian Ethics and Social Policy*. There he defended natural law ("a moral law of nature that can be known apart from revelation").[29] He admitted that some schools, notably many Roman Catholic moralists, conceptualized the natural law "in too static and precise terms" while claiming to be able to apply it to concrete situations in a disinterestedly Christian manner.[30]

Yet Bennett maintained that natural law concepts, as he defined them, were of great value since "it is necessary for Christians and non-Christians to co-operate on practical issues in society."[31] As the theoretical basis for this co-operation he affirmed the existence of "a moral order that can be known

[26] Bennett, "Moral Landmarks in a Time of Confusion" in *Christendom*, I (1935), p. 69. Much of this article is stated in more popular form in *CAOW*.

[27] *Ibid.*, pp. 68–69.

[28] *Ibid.*, pp. 70–77. In "The Christian's Ethical Decision" (1940) intuition was eliminated.

[29] *CESP*, pp. 116–117.

[30] *CESP*, p. 40. By the mid-1960's he no longer thought this was a valid charge against Roman Catholicism. Of course Catholicism had changed in the interim.

[31] *CESP*, p. 119.

with varying degrees of clarity apart from revelation." And the book concludes with the affirmation that it is a

. . . mistake to deny that Christian moral conviction overlaps with a broader knowledge of the moral order that confronts Christians and non-Christians alike, and which, if they fail to heed it, will bring down upon both a common impoverishment of life or a common destruction.[32]

Evidently Bennett was making two similar but subtly different claims. First, and deriving both from his earlier writings on ethics and from his overall philosophical position, the onto-logical claim that there exist moral criteria knowable apart from any revelation—criteria which have a religious or, more spe-cifically, Christian sanction. Second, the historical claim that there is in fact a body of social principles which Christians and non-Christians share and which, therefore, can serve as a basis for political debate. These two claims are different in important respects. The first or ontological one makes it incumbent on a theorist to justify at least some of his social principles on grounds other than revelation; the latter historical one does not. The first claim raises questions about the relation of revealed to natural knowledge; the latter does not. In a word, the first raises epistemological and metaphysical problems which the second avoids.

Only the latter claim (that Christians and non-Christians share social principles) is necessary if the appeal to "natural law" is done for the sake of co-operation. Thus Professor Bennett's writings, at least since *Christians and the State* (1958), take the form of defending the latter thesis. To that thesis, the existence of a moral consensus, this chapter must turn in conclusion.

In *Christians and the State* Bennett argues that we do not face the alternative of either skepticism or the deduction of certain universally acceptable moral principles. Instead the

[32] *CESP,* pp. 120 and 123.

religio-moral translator can point to the existence in our society of certain moral convictions which, whatever their origin, are in fact defended apart from the Christian revelation. There is, at least in the society of the United States, "an overlapping in moral awareness and conviction between Christians and non-Christians."[33] This overlapping is called a "moral consensus." It is the equivalent of the idea of natural law insofar as it includes principles the actual public of the United States can acknowledge:

This conception of the overlapping of the moral awareness and convictions of Christians and non-Christians allows the Christian ethic to have its own grounding in revelation, its own motivation in response to the love of God, its own refinement and expansion through the sensitivity that is the fruit of Christian love. It allows for parallel contexts of faith which support the ethical awareness and convictions of non-Christians.[34]

In other words, this natural law is "natural" in a historical sense. That which we agree on *is* the natural law.[35] Natural law cannot be separated from the commands of love.[36] Thus, on these terms, when one makes the translation from love into broad criteria for social policy, he is not giving Christian sanction to principles justified apart from revelation. All viable social principles are, from this point of view, translations from one faith or other. Confidence in a social reason which could transcend the commitments of a given standpoint has waned.

[33] *CS*, p. 15.

[34] *CS*, pp. 14–17.

[35] Failure to observe this definition leads Joseph Fletcher to say with reference to Bennett "There is something strange in the persistent notion that natural law still provides common ground with non-theological social thought, when in fact it has just the opposite effect." ("Anglican Theology and the Ethics of Natural Law" in *Christian Social Ethics in a Changing World,* ed. John C. Bennett, p. 319). Since *Christians and the State* Bennett has clearly not meant that traditional natural law concepts provide a common ground. He means to define the natural law as the common ground that, in fact, exists.

[36] Bennett, "Principles and the Context" (1961), p. 7.

The notion that there might be a general political logic has disappeared.

What is retained from Bennett's earlier views is the conviction that Christians must translate their political views into terms that all the members of their society will understand. What makes this possible, however, is not the presence of an ontological order but the existence of a moral consensus in society. The consensus is composed of "a recognition of some necessary conditions for a viable social order . . . criteria which are widely recognized to have claims upon us."[37] This consensus, in the United States, involves commitment to such broad criteria as equality, freedom, justice, and personal integrity.[38]

How to explain the existence of this national consensus? Following Eduard Heimann, Bennett holds that it exists because the various American faiths are all biblical.[39] For example, it is because Protestants, Roman Catholics, and Jews all value the documents of the Old Testament (which stress the transcendence of God) that they can unite in rejecting national idolatry.[40] In general, ". . . on the broader issues of social justice, economic life, and foreign policy there are no controversies between the religious communities as such."[41]

Bennett does not mean to suggest by this appeal to history that the consensus cannot be changed. Quite the contrary. Improvement of the consensus is the role of the churches. The consensus "needs to be renewed and corrected by the historic faiths in their fullness." The communities of faith should be true to themselves. They should be "dynamic" with respect to the common life. Indeed:

[37] Bennett, "Christian Ethics and National Conscience," Sixth Annual Alexander Graham Bell Lecture (Boston, 1964), p. 8.
[38] CS, pp. 17–20; see below, chapter 6.
[39] Review of Leo Pfeffer, *Creeds in Competition* in *The Christian Century*, LXXVI (April 15, 1959), p. 454.
[40] Bennett, "Church and State," *New Frontiers of Christianity*, ed. Ralph A. Raughley (New York, 1962), p. 182.
[41] *WCMPD*, p. 98.

. . . the primary task of our religious communities and institutions is to raise the level of the national consensus. It is this which may create better possibilities for political decision. It means a more sensitive public conscience on the most important issues.[42]

On the other hand, it is obviously possible as Bennett recognizes that there will be those whose ultimate commitments are divergent from those of the historic faiths and to whom this "natural law" can make no appeal. The national or cultural consensus cannot serve as a basis for co-operation among *all* men. Not all religions converge on the moral plane—Hinduism and Islam do not, for example. Even in American society there are marginal tendencies, such as that represented by the American NAZI party, which are cut off from correction.[43] That is, they may be able to discuss the sorts of general values making up the consensus, but they do not see these values in the appropriate context. Thus they are likely to misunderstand them.

These inevitable characteristics of the consensus proposal raise a fundamental difficulty for Bennett's theory. For it is surely incongruous to hold that particular religious bodies may engage in pre-political action to raise and correct the national consensus, while at the same time justifying the appeal to consensus on the grounds that it includes values everyone acknowledges. The fact that many citizens are members of no religious communities illustrates the incongruity most sharply. Anything a church does to "raise" the consensus makes it less of a consensus from such a citizen's point of view.

[42] Bennett, "The Religious Concern With Politics," a pamphlet published by the National Conference on Christians and Jews (New York, 1963), p. 4.

[43] Bennett, "Christian Ethics and the National Conscience" (1964), p. 18; cf. Bennett, "Church and State" (1962), p. 192: "I think we should recognize that the complexities of the cultural situation and of the mysteries of human personality are such that a man who has no tie with any of the historic religious faiths may *nevertheless* have the integrity and the moral commitments and the spiritual perspectives that would make him a good President" (emphasis added).

At this point it is important to see that the problem is a logical outgrowth of Bennett's constant concern that religious concepts be translated before they be politically used. The difficulty with the theory lies in the fact that political concepts have a logic of their own. Bennett is committed to preserving the integrity of that logic, but he has also always wanted to assert the relevance of religion to politics. He has wanted to say that there is a characteristic result when, for example, love is expressed as justice—and that the arrangement of justice and freedom must be determined with respect to consequences for human welfare. In other words, he has always held that the Christian's understanding of a concept like justice should have both religious and political components.

Consequently the possibility of conflict between these two components has always been an implicit problem in his thought. It becomes explicit in his recent thought in the possibility of conflict between the consensus of the church (the religious component) and the consensus of the country (the political component). We must now turn our attention to the church: what it is and how it forms its consensus.

4. WHAT THE CHURCH IS

Bennett has not wanted to confine the activity of God and the human response to it within some institutional structure. ". . . God does not give His grace only to those who know Him," he wrote in his first book. "It is mediated by all true affection, by the joys of family life . . . by devotion to any high cause . . . by the suffering which purifies and deepens life."[1] On the other hand, and equally early in his career, Bennett said that the world "needs" the church. In the present state of cultural decay, he wrote in 1935, ". . . the things for which the Church stands are the only things left to give wholeness to life." Therefore, ". . . if the Christian faith in God is no illusion, then the world apart from the Church is a strange caricature of the real world. It has lost its true direction, its sense of proportion, and people live in a narrow segment of their real environment."[2]

The church is necessary in two ways. In the first place it, along with the home and presumably other social bodies, may be an environment in which salvation becomes actual. This is because it, as well as they, may be a community of love and awareness of God; it is not because of some magic sacramental power possessed by the church.[3]

In fact, as a human community, the church knows itself to be a company of sinners. It has been and continues to be

[1] *SS*, pp. 176–177.
[2] Bennett, "The World Needs the Church," *The Younger Churchmen Look at the Church*, ed. Ralph Read (New York, 1935), pp. 20–21.
[3] Bennett, "Christian Conception of Man" (1942), p. 193.

apostate in many ways. The great error of Catholicism at some times and places has been the pretension that the church and its policies were somehow exempt from sinning.[4] The church's greatest temptation is to confuse the divine and human aspects of its life.[5] It must recognize that it is human and sinful. Whatever great affirmations are to be made about the church, its sins must be acknowledged with total frankness.[6] It is by no means to be equated with the kingdom of God.[7]

Yet, in the second place, the fact that the church knows about salvation gives it great strength. This knowledge provides it with an essential relationship to something beyond itself by which it is judged. The definiteness of the perspective makes clear that the church knows an external authority. When the church is most true to itself it "points beyond itself" to that which judges it.[8] Because the church has a self-conscious relationship to revelation it has a "self-righting" power or tendency.[9] This certainly does not mean that the church cannot err. It does suggest that the church's confession provides the best resource for its correction.[10]

Consequently, the church is a kind of intellectual environment which can be of great benefit to the individual Christian. He would be helpless in the face of pagan and other influences if the ethos of the church were not there to succor him. This

[4] *Ibid.*, p. 200.
[5] Bennett, "The Limitations of the Church," *The Gospel, the Church, and the World*, ed. Kenneth S. Latourette (New York, 1946), p. 135.
[6] *CR*, p. 140.
[7] Bennett, "The Forms of Ecumenical Christianity," *Toward World-Wide Christianity*, ed. O. Frederick Nolde (New York, 1946), pp. 63–64.
[8] See, for example, *CS*, pp. 200–203.
[9] This phraseology is from *SS*, p. 171; the power involved has sometimes been attributed to the Holy Spirit, as in Bennett, "The Limitations of the Church" (1946).
[10] *FPCP*, p. 35: "There is no reason for the Christian community, in spite of all its own sins and distortions, to lose its identity as the bearer of the sources of its own correction; and I doubt if the secular world has sources of correction that can take the place of those that come through God's revelation in Christ."

87

becomes more and more vividly true as the world becomes more and more hostile to Christianity; it is especially true in a totalitarian state.[11]

Jesus is the source of the church's power. In Bennett's view, as we have seen, Jesus did not complete some supernatural act. But he is the center of the movement of redemption; his work is a persuasive influence mediated by the church. In his life and death one can see:

> . . . the beginning of a new environment for humanity. Because of what Jesus did, the world is a radically different place in the sense that the influences and stimuli that surround the soul from birth are radically different. This does not mean that the secular order is necessarily better, but that within the world there is another order which is never entirely controlled by the secular order, an order which is what it is because of the works of Christ.[12]

The community founded by Jesus is the "scaffolding for an order of life which can exist now in the world in spite of evil and tragedy."[13]

Thus the community which Jesus brought into being, the church, is "a community in which God is at work in a special way for the redemption of the world," a community which mediates the grace and truth which were in Christ to future generations.[14] The church is the movement in which "God is working most clearly to lift the level of the life of men";[15] the

[11] See Bennett, "Forms of Ecumenical Christianity" (1946), p. 60.

[12] *CR*, p. 136; for Bennett the influence of the Christian movement extends outside the church. Thus, although: "It is through the Christian fellowship that we are influenced by Christ," it is also true that: ". . . insofar as the spiritual climate has been moulded by Christianity, we find Christ mediated in at least a dim way by persons and movements outside the Church" (*CR*, p. 137). The main reason for suggesting that Bennett still holds these views is their congruence with things he now says about the church. Also, of course, he has never retracted these affirmations.

[13] Bennett, "Christianity and Social Salvation" (1938), p. 9.

[14] Bennett, "Concern for Theology" in *Commonweal*, LXXVIII (1963), p. 420.

[15] *CAOW*, p. 14.

"one strand of history in which God has been most clearly at work for human redemption."[16] God definitely works elsewhere, even to correct the church, but the redemptive activity of God has been "concentrated" in it.[17] Therefore, if Christianity as a view of the world (the Christian perspective) is true, then the church is uniquely necessary; secular substitutes for the church and its perspective are based on inadequate views of human needs.[18]

If this is *what* the church truly is, *where* is it? In Bennett's view it is present within the visible and imperfect churches.[19] It is not invisible since it consists of actual men and women but it is different from the list of the membership of the churches. It is possible that there are institutions and individuals that call themselves part of the true church and yet really are not to be included.[20]

The institutional church is not identical with the true church, but "it is chiefly through these same institutions and congregations that the new community becomes embodied. . . . [the churches] have formed the banks between which the continuous stream of Christian life has moved until it reaches us. The Church is an earthen vessel that carries the greatest treasure and it is an indispensable vessel if the treasure is to come near us."[21] One can speak with confidence of "the Christian community within the Churches" which is the tangible historical result of the new beginning in Jesus Christ.[22] The true church is "embodied in" the churches.[23]

[16] Bennett, "The Outlook for Theology" (1941), p. 352.

[17] Bennett uses this phrase in writings as far apart in time as "The Forms of Ecumenical Christianity" (1946), pp. 61 and 63 and *FPCP* (1966), p. 49.

[18] *CR,* p. 139; note the consistency of this with Bennett's "theology" discussed in chapter 1.

[19] See, for example, Bennett, "The Limitations of the Church" (1946), p. 135.

[20] Bennett, "The Forms of Ecumenical Christianity" (1946), p. 64.

[21] *CCT* (1948–62), pp. 129–130.

[22] *Ibid.,* p. 131.

[23] *CR,* pp. 141–142.

The true church so contained has two characteristics. First, it is universal; second, it is morally responsible.

"The Church is not, and can never be, the Church of a local community," wrote J. H. Oldham in 1938. "The Church in any particular locality is part of a universal community and is known to be such."[24] This was said to be the opinion of several speakers at the Oxford Conference of 1937, and it is a conviction that John C. Bennett, who was deeply impressed by that conference, has never forsaken.

"The Church in one nation," he wrote in 1958, "is a part of a universal Christian community and when it does not live as a loyal part of that whole, it ceases to be a Christian Church."[25] The same principle holds within the nation. Local congregations, despite their irreplaceable function, cannot live in isolation. Rather, such congregations must live "as a part of a larger unit of the Church which is racially and socially inclusive in its membership."[26]

According to Bennett, local or regional church units are most often those groups "most determined by a particular culture." To counteract that cultural determination these church units should be aware of "many types of experience and diverse cultural pressures."[27] Or, again:

. . . local churches because they tend to reflect the limited interests and prejudices of a particular residential area, must depend for inspiration and correction on larger units of the Church.[28]

[24] Joseph H. Oldham, "Introduction," *Oxford Conference Report*, ed. J. H. Oldham (1937), p. 22.
[25] *CS*, p. 183; cf. *WCMPD*, p. 107: ". . . no Church is a true Church unless it lives as a part of a universal Church. The Roman Catholic knows where the center of that universal Church is; the Protestant may seem vague at this point."
[26] Bennett, "Inaugural Address as President of Union Seminary" (1964), p. 406.
[27] Bennett, "Farewell Address" (unpublished) given at the Union Theological Seminary Commencement 1965, p. 4.
[28] Bennett, "The Church as Prophetic Critic" in *The Christian Century*, LXXXI (January 6, 1954), p. 10.

The partial and incomplete perspectives of individuals "need to be checked by various forms of corporate prophetic teaching."[29]

Bennett's explanation for the "primacy"[30] of more socially inclusive units of the church centers around the crucial role of the Christian perspective. For Bennett it is the possession of the perspective which differentiates the church from other communities. Where the true perspective is, there, to a certain extent (see below), is the true church. Where is the true perspective? Who has it? Bennett is convinced that no ideology can be identified with it, but he thinks that there is a more or less reliable way of approximating the perspective.

The way which Professor Bennett defends is the way of dialogue:

. . . there is no Christian way to wisdom that does not take account of the sinful distortion and the finiteness of our minds. The best chance for a Christian judgment to emerge from these situations comes when partial or one-sided views are expressed in such a way as to correct each other . . .[31]

This dialogue is not existential or mystical but simple, personal confrontation. Through it provincialism and cultural biases will be overcome. People will learn to see themselves as others see them and will, literally, gain "perspective" on their views. The new perspective, formed on the basis of discussion, argument, and agreement, is a *consensus*.

What is the basis of Professor Bennett's faith in dialogue? On the one hand, we must remember that for him the Christian perspective is a view of the world which must be confirmed by experience and the view which most adequately explains experience. Since this is the case, it follows that the more ex-

---

[29] Bennett, "Principles and the Context" (1961), p. 20.

[30] *CS*, p. 277. In "Authority in Christian Social Ethics" (1967), pp. 13–14 Bennett says: ". . . it is essential that judgements about controversial social issues be made at a level at which those who participate come from many social groups and reflect diverse experiences."

[31] *WCMPD*, p. 105.

91

perience brought to bear on the perspective, the greater the likelihood that it will be both valid and true.

On the other hand, many of the theologians contemporary with Bennett (not least Reinhold Niebuhr and H. Richard Niebuhr) held that one's faith must be understood to be inseparable from one's historically conditioned standpoint. For these men the perspective of faith was the point of view on the ultimate held by one particular group at one particular time. If that is the case, Bennett seems to ask, why not amalgamate our perspectives and get the best, albeit still finite, point of view possible? If the limitations on one's perspective are the product of one's social experience, it would seem to follow that the best way to transcend these limitations would be to broaden one's range of experience. Given that we can only approach God from a limited point of view, let us try to assume the point of view in which the light of truth is refracted as little as possible.

The consensus reached by a group represents just such a point of view. The consensus is not arrived at by "counting heads,"[32] or by "a kind of Gallup Poll of the constituency of the churches."[33] It is not the view of the majority. It must be formed by "processes that bring together both clergy and laity, persons of different social background and bias, experts in different fields in the context of the Church, and this means in the context of the Church's international experience."[34]

It is absolutely crucial that the consensus be the product of an international body, for only then are real differences of cultural outlook transcended. The new relationships that an international community makes possible are irreplaceable in this connection. That is why Professor Bennett has consistently made great claims for the World Council of Churches.

For Professor Bennett a World Council assembly is "the occasion on which the world-wide community of Christians

[32] Bennett, "Authority in Christian Social Ethics" (1967), p. 12.
[33] FPCP, pp. 155–156.
[34] Bennett, "Amsterdam and the Social Crisis" in The Christian Century, LXV (Janaury 9, 1948), p. 571.

becomes most visible, becomes a tangible reality."[35] In the World Council one can see "a world-wide Christian community coming into being," a community which "points beyond all the various denominational authorities whether they acknowledge it or not."[36] The experience of dialogue that happens in these assemblies reveals the church "at its best";[37] it is "a fact which should determine our thinking about the Church even if we have to accept it on the testimony of others."[38]

Because the World Council of Churches represents the forum in which the Christian perspective can best be approximated, the consensus it reaches, especially about ethical questions, becomes very important for Professor Bennett. Bennett himself has been an important shaper of that consensus. He has attended every major (and most of the minor) ecumenical conferences since Oxford in 1937. At most of these he has had an official position, and he has written many of the reports.

More important than Professor Bennett's participation in these conferences, however, is the use he makes of the reports in his own writing. There the reports are copiously cited. As we will see below, Bennett's most consistent and natural way of proving a point is by an appeal to the consensus of the ecumenical community. When he looks for an authority beyond his own reflections he looks to the ecumenical consensus, not to a text of scripture or to a fully worked out social philosophy. Of course his own theologizing affects the way Bennett tries to form the consensus, but he has much less faith in private theories than in the ecumenical community.

Not only is this method of working a natural outgrowth of Professor Bennett's personally modest character, it is also quite consistent with his stress on humility. The appeal to

[35] Bennett, "Report from New Delhi" in *The Union Seminary Quarterly Review*, XVII, No. 2 (January, 1962); cf. *CS*, p. 200 and "Social Issues at New Delhi" in *Christianity and Crisis*, XXI, No. 18 (October 30, 1961), p. 194.

[36] Bennett, "View of Authority in the Church" (1964), p. 217.

[37] Bennett, "The Forms of Ecumenical Christianity" (1946), p. 62.

[38] *CR*, p. 155.

consensus represents Bennett's faith in people and discussion, rather than in grand theological schemes. It represents his awareness that any consistent conceptual link between theology and political philosophy is inevitably partial and arbitrary. Thus, in a sense, the consensus serves the same function in his thought that the love-justice dialectic does in the thought of Reinhold Niebuhr: it gives him a concrete point of departure for his political reflections.

For Bennett there can be no thought of absolutizing any one set of theological or political principles. And his importance, relative to his contemporaries, surely lies in just this fact. He is aware, as they did not always seem to be, that the necessities of political and theological discourse are different. Thus he does not subordinate or subsume political principles under theological ones. He radically frees political principles from that kind of heteronomy. The relationship between faith and ethics is one of translation.

But, as Bennett's uses of the ecumenical consensus inevitably suggest, his own theory is not without its difficulties. If he does not absolutize a set of ideas or a set of insights, he does tend to put unqualified confidence in the deliberations of a particular social body.

There are general considerations which force him to do this. A religious community can never be satisfied with the simple assertion that the perspective must be translated into directives for action. In the first place, the absolute aspect of a person's religious loyalties means that a religious person inevitably wants definite moral guidance from his religion. The intensity of religion tends to require universal extensity. In the second place, the actual demands of a social institution which wants to have a characteristic impact on society require the formulation of a specific set of ethical principles. A religious moralist, therefore, must produce a rather concrete and specific ethic. And, in the context of Bennett's thought, the needed definiteness can only come from one place: the world church.

What in fact are the difficulties with the role that Bennett

94

assigns to the ecumenical community? In the first place, the difficulties with saying that Christian social insight emerges from ecumenical dialogue seem to be obvious. It is hard to reconcile such a statement with the doctrine of sin, so long as sin is different from finitude. Theologians usually assert that sin distorts our perception of truth, and that the most one can hope for in ecumenical dialogue is that finitude, not sin, be overcome. If one holds that both sinful and finite distortions of truth are overcome in the ecumenical setting, then he is implying that finitude of experience is the essence of sin, and not just a forum in which it manifests itself. This is a hard affirmation to reconcile with the anthropology of *The Nature and Destiny of Man*—which, as I argued in chapter 1, Bennett has accepted since the early 1940's. Yet if one says that finitude and not sin is overcome in dialogue, he must be able to explain how the distortions of one kind differ from those of the other. Further, in point of fact, he would have to assume that the distortions caused by finitude are much more significant than those caused by sin in order to justify giving great weight to ecumenical literature and discussion.[39]

On a second level, it seems questionable to argue that social distortions are overcome in ecumenical dialogue. The fact that many men are in possession of half-truths does not mean that in conversation they will produce the whole of the truth. Their half-truths may in fact cancel each other out. Instead of clarifying the issues they may further distort them. It is especially problematic to say that *religious* truth emerges from consensus if religious truth refers to a reality not accessible to public examination and description. Moreover, and surely more telling to Bennett's own purposes, is the fact that socially heterogeneous religious bodies do not necessarily more closely approximate what many of us take to be Christian truth than do parochial ones.

Bennett has been misled by the success he has had in appeal-

[39] Cf. Bennett, "The Limitations of the Church" (1946), pp. 138–142.

ing to the World Council community against American economic and international provincialism. That success has blinded him to the obvious fact that an appeal to a larger unit of the church may be an appeal to the parochial, or even to the demonic. What if various experimental and commendable ministries in, for instance, New York City, had to appeal to larger units of the American church to sanction their practices? Can one but doubt that the result would be to inhibit the social work of the church? The primacy of larger units of the church is a very dangerous principle indeed for a Protestant theologian.

In the second place, even if one were to grant that the Christian social truth emerged as the product of the ecumenical consensus, Bennett's claims make the political status of the ecumenical consensus very uncertain. In order to fully appreciate this problem, several things must be kept in mind. The first of these is that for Professor Bennett the perspective defended by the consensus of the ecumenical community tends to be the best perspective on human affairs.

Bennett neither says nor implies that the ecumenical consensus cannot err. What is of interest at this point is to notice that he has reason to rely on it more than on the consensus of other groups. Earlier in this chapter we noted his claims for the uniqueness of the church. They are still present in his writings since his formulation of the national consensus proposal. The idea that proposal embodies is that social decisions must be made with reference to a common morality. Nevertheless:

. . . the Christian revelation provides the most adequate context for all but the most obviously prudential elements in the common morality. The unity of humanity as I have presented it and as it is widely affirmed is a precarious conviction if all men are not seen in their relationship to God as creator and redeemer. Freedom can be best understood ultimately as the freedom of the person who belongs wholly to no social group, who is a citizen of two cities, who is responsible to God. Christian faith provides not only the most adequate grounding for what is true in the common morality

96

but also the motives for obedience which in the long run are most dependable.[40]

Furthermore, there is a real connection between the revelation of God in Christ and the deliberations of the ecumenical Christian community. According to Professor Bennett the members of the ecumenical community live under the revelation of God in Christ which "transcends and corrects every purpose which men have for their societies" and "they can be helped by one another in this correction out of their contrasting experiences."[41] The revelation of God in Christ is the best revelation; it is approximated through ecumenical dialogue; therefore, ecumenical dialogue approximates the best revelation or the best perspective.

Finally, this perspective is associated with the views of a particular group within national societies. That group is the Christian ministry.

The minister has a unique social role in that he is detached from many class biases.[42] Consequently: ". . . the clergy have an opportunity that most laymen do not have to become familiar with all the guidance that Christian teaching can bring from the past to the present, from the larger Church to the local Church."[43] Further, the church's consensus is not confined to that which every Christian can affirm:

It is rather a trend of thinking that characterizes those who take initiative in thought and in leadership and whose responsibility it

[40] *CS*, pp. 22–23; cf. Bennett's pamphlet, "Christian Ethics and the National Conscience," Sixth Annual Alexander Graham Bell Lecture, on "Man's Communication to Man" (Boston, 1964), p. 24: "If Christians believe that some of these common convictions would not exist if it were not for the influence of Christ upon the culture, they may have a case for this. There are times for saying this and times for refraining from saying it and to work with those who share the same goals without making special claims and with thanks to God that those others are there."

[41] Bennett, "Demand for Freedom and Justice" (1959), p. 334.

[42] Bennett, "Inaugural Address" in *Union Theological Seminary Alumni Bulletin*, XIX, No. 1 (December, 1943), p. 4.

[43] *CESP*, p. 105.

is to emphasize the relationship of current thinking to the sources of the revelation, and who are able to transcend to some extent local and even national and cultural pressures.[44]

Although contributors to the consensus will include the laity and experts in various fields of action, it is generally recognized that ". . . those whose training and life work have caused them to concentrate on the distinctively Christian sources of wisdom should have a very important role in decisions."[45]

The same point is sometimes formulated in ways not too flattering to the local clergy:

As one moves away from the local churches to the leadership of the larger units of the Church, one finds a different atmosphere, in which there is a definite effort to counteract the pressure of class interests, and to find distinctively Christian guidance concerning controversial social issues.[46]

But the basic principle remains the same: ". . . the clergy . . . have a chance to transcend local pressures because of their training and because of their relationships and because of the conditions of their job (less dependent on the local situation for status and economic security than most people)." Their competence is limited, of course, since, "Ordination does not of itself confer wisdom on any subject." Nevertheless, although the danger of clericalism is real, ". . . the Church needs to be protected against domination by the grassroots where little specifically Christian insight on social ethics has penetrated. . . ."[47]

[44] Bennett, "Protestant Ethics and Population Control" (1959), p. 455.

[45] CS, pp. 275–276. He does add: "I am advocating no closed clique of clergy and of the comparatively few laymen 'who get around' as the ultimate Protestant authority!" (p. 278).

[46] Bennett, "Christian Ethics and Forms of Economic Power," Christian Values and Economic Life, eds. John C. Bennett et al. (New York, 1954), p. 238.

[47] Bennett, "Authority in Christian Social Ethics" (1967), pp. 14–15.

Of course Bennett does not mean this line of argument to suggest the superior virtue of the Christian clergy. It is his way of explaining their authority in sociological terms. Membership in the ecumenical community provides a clergyman with a relationship involving a certain freedom from economic, political and social vested interests. This degree of freedom is intensified as the characteristically Christian influences are intensified and the cultural vested interests decrease. This happens as the environment in which one operates shifts from the congregation to the church as an international whole.

In other words, as one moves into an ethos that is more and more influenced by differing Christian influences, one must move out of a less fortunately conditioned environment. One begins to *substitute* the Christian perspective for a nationally or socially conditioned one. That is the reason that Bennett can put great faith in the reports of the World Council.

When we remember that Professor Bennett suggests that the Christian perspective is superior to other religious perspectives, the difficulties of this theory should be apparent. It implicitly places the World Council of Churches in the role of an Ideal Observer on political debate, for that body is loyal to the perspective that is most valid and true and, further, it embodies the mechanism in which that perspective is approximated.

It is not at all clear how Professor Bennett might qualify his views so as to avoid this implication. There are two crucial affirmations which lead up to it. The first of these is that discussion, indeed, the discussions of a particular group, approximate the Christian perspective. The second is that a view of the world which is more Christian is for that very reason politically more just. For Bennett being Christian and being socially ideal are indistinguishable; the definition of need produced by the consensus is more Christian precisely because it emerges from the interaction of different social standpoints. It is religiously important because it is socially and politically nonpartisan.

The first of these affirmations (about the role of discussion) has already been considered. What about the second? Obviously one of the great strengths of Professor Bennett's thought is the insistence that the connection between religious and political ideas be made in a sophisticated way. He minimizes the conceptual aspect of this connection and stresses the procedural aspect: the perspective suggests that need must be assuaged; the consensus determines what is needed. The only *concept* linking the two sides (religious and political) is the concept of need.

But that link is a vital one. As was argued above, all of Bennett's theological affirmations are made with social action in view. They all tend to represent concepts which could be integral parts of a consensus. In a word, the fact that perspective will be used as a basis for political philosophy obviously affects what it will include. On the other hand, Bennett clearly does not mean that the consensus of the ecumenical community can ignore the Christian theological perspective. Indeed, he says that the perspective must be *translated* into political policy. To ignore this linkage, this reciprocal interaction, between faith and politics would be to opt for the irrelevance of religion to policy, a course Bennett obviously rejects.

If Bennett were to deny this linkage, if he were to suggest that statements of faith, while they must be true, need not be socially valid, he could avoid the implication that the ecumenical Christian community maintains a privileged political standpoint. He could say, in effect, that the Christian perspective is uniquely true and that dialogue is the way the perspective is approximated but he could deny that the perspective so discovered has any political validity whatsoever. In other words he could retain his faith in dialogue (which, as we have seen, is questionable) if he were to distinguish even more radically the norms and function of religious language and communities from the norms and function of political language and communities.

Bennett goes a long way in this direction, further, I think, than any of his contemporaries. But he remained preoccupied

100

with a problem set for his generation by Reinhold Niebuhr: how to formulate a "Christian perspective" that would include propositions that are both religiously adequate and politically usable. The difficulty with this enterprise is that the desiderata of faith are different from those of politics: faith requires absolute intensity and passion; politics requires compromise. Bennett sees this difficulty; he tries to modify Reinhold Niebuhr's theology to get around it. Yet the result is a kind of unguarded reliance on the World Council of Churches—a reliance which places that body in a role no community could fulfill. If that is so, the fundamental lesson to be learned may be that the original objective—the statement of a socio-religious perspective—was mistakenly chosen.

However that may be, nothing that has been said should suggest that Bennett regards church union (consensus) as a panacea. The possibility remains that the church could say the right thing but be apostate. The church should not only have true knowledge; she should be a group which is saved and saving. Bennett thinks that some kind of international federation would be of value but not a full corporate union in which the rights of minorities might be compromised.[48] The goal of ecumenical activity is not a "monolithic ecclesiastical institution."[49] There is no guarantee that the vast ecclesiastical machine that would result from full church union would be "less cautious than the existing denominations."[50]

Bennett's rejection of ecumenicism as a cure for all the ills of the church became explicit in a disagreement with Charles Clayton Morrison. Morrison referred to the church as the revelation in history of "the presence, the character, and the purpose of God." The church, the "medium of God's self-

[48] Bennett, "The Forms of Ecumenical Christianity" (1946), p. 73.
[49] Bennett, "Ecumenical Theology: Comment on Professor Pauck's Paper" in the *Journal of Religion*, XXV, No. 4 (October, 1945), p. 275.
[50] Bennett, Review of Morrison's book *The Social Gospel and the Christian Cultus* in *The World Tomorrow*, XVI (1933), p. 621.

disclosure in history," was a particular human community as old as the origins of the Hebrew people but now supraracial and inclusive.[51] It confessed itself to be the revelation of the divine presence and its "Great Apostasy" was its:

. . . subordination of the *koinonia,* the organic fellowship of the Christian community, to the claims of doctrine, or organization, or tradition, or Bible or personal experience.[52]

For Morrison, the ecumenical movement represented a means of altering the institutional forms of Christianity so that they truly expressed the reality of the body of Christ. The true church was there within the existing churches but it had lost its proper form. That form could be realized through the formation of an ecumenical polity. A church so unified would be the true church.

For Professor Bennett, however, the unity of perspective which ecumenism produces provides no guarantee of actual faithfulness. Unity is the crucial way of encouraging the church to a faithful confession, it is true. But, always, the possibility remains that a united church might be apostate in the sense that it might cease to *be* a community of loving concern for the needs and welfare of the world. Unity, for Bennett, is not an end in itself; it is a means to an end. He could be sympathetic for Morrison's interest in the church, even for some of the claims he made for it. But: "Unity without prophetic criticism of the church and the world would be little gain."[53] The church does not exist to preserve itself but to respond to need, to work for the public welfare. A church which did not do those things would be apostate, however impressively united it might be. Material needs and conditions can impede salvation. On the other hand, salvation expresses itself in moral action. Therefore the true company of the saved must be moral.

[51] Morrison, *What is Christianity?* (1940), pp. 57 and 66–67.
[52] *Ibid.,* p. 263; cf. pp. 67 and 276ff.
[53] Review of *What is Christianity?* (1941), p. 117; cf. "A Changed Liberal" (1939), p. 181.

102

This is true in, at least, three senses. First, there is a kind of moral test for salvation and church membership. It is clear to Professor Bennett that those who profess and call themselves Christians are not necessarily the ones who are the furthest advanced toward salvation. Someone who seeks what God wills, even though denying his existence, may be closer to God than someone who praises him in church while defending injustice.[54] Thus, in point of fact, the company of true Christians making up the church is different from the membership of the actual churches. It is inevitable that there will be true disciples outside the flock.

But the real question is, who may the church include? In Bennett's terms the need for dialogue precludes a sectarian exclusivistic church. An overly exclusive church would become self-righteous, lose contact with the community as a whole, and isolate itself from the main body of Christians, thus losing the chance "to be corrected or enriched by the larger fellowship."[55] The church should not be composed of religio-moral virtuosi:

. . . we also need a large rank and file of people in the Church who are capable of being led to the position where they know what the prophet is talking about and where they recognize that there are truths in his message which have a claim upon them.[56]

This suggests that allegiance to a given political or moral standard should not become a criterion for church membership. The church should include both radicals and conservatives, both pacifists and non-pacifists. Christianity, the true church, transcends these precarious technical and political judgments. It includes those who err on this lower level and thus is a company of sinners, not of saints.[57]

[54] *CAOW*, p. 1.
[55] Bennett, "The Limitations of the Church" (1946), p. 137.
[56] Bennett, "New Emphases in Christian Social Teaching" in *Religion in Life*, VII (1938), p. 535.
[57] *Ibid.*, pp. 532–533.

But inclusiveness is one thing and all-inclusiveness is another. Addressing the Oxford Conference, J. H. Oldham had stated that just as the ancient church was able to state which dogmatic views were false, so the modern church should be able to say what social principles are unchristian. Then as now the church could not formulate a comprehensive statement of what she is for. But she could be certain that some things were wrong.[58]

Similarly for Bennett, the members of the church "recognize a definite standard and a definite loyalty in the light of which they are sinners." The existence of this definite standard of loyalty makes Christians a "peculiar people" and it means there are "many who have no place in the Church" who "should be encouraged to eliminate themselves." Although conscientious believers in the use of military force belong in the Church:

. . . the complacent militarist who has a certain type of piety in one compartment of his soul should be brought to see the contradiction between what the Church stands for and what he stands for in public life.[59]

This early article, reflecting as it does Bennett's early social views, represents a basic point he has not since discarded. In

---

[58] J. H. Oldham, "The Function of the Church in Society," *The Church and its Function in Society*, eds. W. A. Visser 'T Hooft and Joseph H. Oldham, pp. 228–229.

[59] Bennett, "New Emphases in Christian Social Teaching" (1938), pp. 533–534. This is in response to Morrison who wrote in *Christendom* in 1938 that the righteousness of the saints was as rags when seen in the "white light that falls upon God's altar." Bennett responded with some passion: "The ideal of anti-semitism, the ideal of a completely regimented society, the ideal of the militant who says that the battlefield is to man what motherhood is to women. . . . do these ideals fare any worse in the white light that falls upon God's altar than the ideal of mutuality among nations, of equal opportunity for all persons regardless of class or race to develop their capacities? . . . to suggest either rhetorically or as a one-sided form of theology that all human ideals are equal before God is moral nihilism and it is a denial that in Christ, who as a man and a teacher, [sic] did not completely transcend all other teachers, the Word was made flesh."

1950 he argued that one could distinguish "conservatives" who were aware of the problems of innovation from "reactionaries" who were committed to the support of the status quo. Whereas the church should include conservatives, Christian communities "should be communities in which the reactionary will come to feel that he is out of place."[60] He wants the church to be inclusive and is aware that loyalty to Christ "is at a level that is prior to and deeper than the particular judgments about public issues which the Churches have made." But how little this means that loyalty to the Church is a non-moral loyalty is suggested by his rationale for distinguishing fundamental from particular loyalties:

If sincere Church members regard themselves as almost excommunicated because of a particular controversial issue . . . the Church might lose contact not only with them but with their children and the chances are that the children will not share their parents' blind spots. Even their wives might differ. The problem of the Church at this point is to take positions carefully and yet seek to understand why these do not commend themselves immediately to many faithful Churchmen as part of their faith.[61]

Bennett's point is not that the church is the sort of society that includes those with radically antithetical social views. Instead it is that the church is not to lose influence by eliminating from its membership people who disagree with its consensus. He insists that the church is in principle a morally committed group, a group formed by a kind of loyalty which has definite social consequences.

Thus, secondly, the socio-moral activity of the church is a historical sign or symptom of its state of health. One reason for thinking of the contemporary period as one of reformation in the church is the fact that its social conscience has been awakened.[62] This return of moral fiber is seen in the resistance

[60] Bennett, Editorial: "The Self-Defeating Attitude of America's 'Reactionaries' " in *Christianity and Crisis*, X, No. 8 (May 15, 1950), p. 58.
[61] Bennett, "Authority in Christian Social Ethics" (1967), pp. 16–17.
[62] *CR*, pp. 149–152.

of the church to tyranny.[63] On the other hand, the rise of Communism and other non-Christian social movements is a symptom of the ill health of the nineteenth-century church which had become allied with the privileged classes against the workers.[64] A healthy, true, and faithful church is a morally committed and active church.

Consequently, third, when the church is true to itself it acknowledges its social and moral responsibility. By its very commission, the church "has responsibility for the life of society as a whole. It is called to mediate the love and the judgment of God to every phase of human life."[65] Where there is need not met the church must involve itself. In fact it has not chosen to stand aloof but has helped to tame and refine the human race, nourished prophetic minorities, and helped people relate themselves to God.[66]

From early in his career Bennett has held that the primary way in which the church should take social responsibility is by exposing our moral rationalizations, by being an authority on the ways in which ideals and religious faith are prostituted.[67] It should reveal to its members the extent to which they are controlled by class interests and national passions, the roots of social evil in their own hearts.[68] It must extend the area in which people feel a genuine sense of sin and encourage the development of an inner attitude which fits the situation of their actual responsibility.[69] In a word, the true church will raise the neglected questions and force society to confront the victims of its policies. Exactly what this raising of questions involves will be the subject of the next chapter.

[63] See Bennett, "Forms of Ecumenical Christianity" (1946), p. 61.
[64] See, for example, Bennett, "The Christian Answer to Communism" (1950), pp. 354–355.
[65] CS, pp. 201–202.
[66] CR, p. 143.
[67] Bennett, "The Religious Foundations" (1937), pp. 17–20.
[68] Bennett, "New Emphases in Christian Social Teaching" (1938), p. 529.
[69] Bennett, "The Causes of Social Evil" (1938), pp. 193–194.

5. WHAT THE CHURCH DOES

Bishop McConnell, reviewing *Social Salvation,* said that he wished that Bennett had stressed more the role of the churches as active social entities, "with a power to bring out of the members acting together possibilities to which they do not attain acting separately."[1] Whether that is a fair criticism of that early book is questionable, but it is certain that underemphasis on the social role of the church is not a characteristic of Bennett's thought since that time.

Since 1941 Bennett has insisted that there are two kinds of subjects of Christian responsibility; two kinds of agents who can be praised or blamed. The first of these is, of course, the individual Christian. He must make his personal decisions for himself. Yet he acts in a society which inevitably corrupts the fruit of his action. Thus, on the social level "as I have been coming to see more and more clearly, there is a sense in which the unit of decision is not the individual at all but the Church."[2] The church which includes those who decide in many different ways will be able to produce a "more balanced witness."

Christian action is not simply an individual matter; it is an affair of the church. The community of which he is a part should aid the individual's response to human need:

[1] Francis J. McConnell, Review of *Social Salvation* in *Christendom,* I (1935), p. 186. The review is colorful and enthusiastic and could have been written without reading the book.
[2] Bennett, "The Christian's Ethical Decision" (1940), pp. 400–401. In "A Changed Liberal" (1939), Bennett put the point rather nicely: "I have become more interested in the possibilities of an awakened Church upon society than in pushing my own political guesses" (p. 180).

The Christian, trained within the Christian Church, must make his own choices in the world, and the possibilities between which he must choose should have more promise because the Christian Church is in the world.[3]

How the church is to act so as to improve the social possibilities is the subject of this chapter. What kind of things is it legitimate for it to do? The Christian perspective, Bennett says, includes an affirmation about the Christian church. The Christian church is the united and socially responsible body of Christians. They want to act for the benefit of human welfare. But the question of strategy remains. What types of actions should the church perform for the sake of welfare?

Bennett's answer to that question makes use of a distinction between direct and indirect action by the church. The terminology used is somewhat misleading since it suggests that the one form of action consists of responding to need oneself while the other form consists of somehow inducing someone else to do it. Thus someone might say that I *directly* hurt someone if I strike him myself while I *indirectly* hurt him if I torment my friend so that my friend strikes him instead. In the first case my action is direct, in the second, indirect. This kind of distinction is suggested by Bennett's terminology with regard to church action.

But it is not the distinction which Bennett has in mind. What he is thinking of is the problem of the commitment of the church itself. He wants to distinguish between actions which directly commit the church as a social unit and those which only indirectly commit it through involving various parts of its membership. To return to the analogy, direct action is like striking my enemy myself; indirect action, rather than being like inducing someone else to do the striking, is like accidentally striking him on the head with the back-swing of a golf club. Indirect action is my action, but it is not in the fullest sense action to which I as a moral unit have committed myself. I re-

[3] *CESP,* p. 115.

main the responsible agent, but I am less culpable (or praise-worthy) than I would be if I simply struck the victim in a straightforward manner.

Perhaps the analogy with the individual case is misleading. On the social level, the formulation of this distinction (without use of the words direct and indirect) which most influenced Bennett was that of J. H. Oldham in his essay preparatory to the Oxford Conference of 1937. There Oldham argued that one can distinguish between the "Church as a society organized for worship and the preaching of the Word" and "the Church as a community of men and women living in the world but committed through faith in Christ to a new outlook on life and a new way of living." The church could be thought of both as a unitary social corporation organized for characteristically religious purposes and, on the other hand, as an aggregation of individual Christians who were members of that corporation. With that distinction in mind:

The witness and action of the Church as an organized society, and as such distinct and separate from other forms of human association, and the witness and action of the Church through its individual members who at the same time in an endless variety of callings participate in the activities of these other associations, are two distinct, though immediately related, questions.[4]

Thus the church might act through the clergy, through its own authorities, or through the laity. These forms of action are quite different. What Christians can and should do is one thing;

---

[4] J. H. Oldham, "The Function of the Church in Society," p. 191. Oldham clearly wanted to stress the role of the laity: ". . . as a rule, in discussing the witness and action of the Church in the corporate life, we tend to think of what can be done by the Church acting in its corporate capacity, whereas, in fact, what can be accomplished by lay men and women actively engaged from day to day in the affairs of the world is incomparably greater in its range, effectiveness and importance. The Church as an organized society stands outside the activities of the social and political life. The Christian laity participate in these activities. Transformation from within is immeasurably more effective than any influence that can be brought to bear from without" (*ibid.*).

what the church as a social entity can and should do is another.[5]

Similarly, Bennett has described the indirect influence of the church as basically "an unintended by-product of Christian worship and of Christian fellowship."[6] To say that the church acts indirectly is to say either that "the Churches are not conscious of a primary intention to influence economic or political decisions" or that "when they are concerned about such decisions they influence society through the activities of their members as citizens."[7] The church's indirect action is action which is not undertaken in a formal sense by the church as a corporate entity.

Direct action, on the other hand, consists primarily of "decisions that are made by official Church bodies for the purpose of influencing public policy either through public opinion or through direct approaches to agencies of government."[8] A pronouncement calling upon *government* to do something is *direct* action because in formulating it the church, as such, has directly acted.

The indirect action of the church is action which is undertaken by individual Christians but not by the church as a whole. The church may be related to it in two ways: in the first place, the church may foster it; in the second place, it may simply live

[5] *Ibid.*, pp. 118–120.

[6] *CESP*, p. 103.

[7] *CS*, p. 278. It must be noted that Bennett has not always used these terms with exactly the same meanings and that the discussion in this chapter is based on the classification given in *Christians and the State* (1958), Chapter 18. For instance in "Enduring Bases of Christian Action" (1943) "direct action" is activity by an individual in response to teaching by the Church while "indirect action" is simply the preservation of fellowship and freedom by the Church as a society (p. 33). Again, in *Christian Ethics and Social Policy* (1946), pp. 99–108, Bennett distinguished between (a) unintentional byproducts (that is, fellowship and freedom as in the earlier work) (b) direct teaching by the Church with action by the individual Christian and (c) action by the Church itself. While this suggests that Bennett has no commitment to a definite terminology, it also shows that these are distinctions he has tried to refine over the years. That is why his most recent classification provides the form for the discussion in this chapter.

[8] *CS*, p. 281.

in the confidence that it will happen. In other words, the indirect action can be something the church strives to bring about or something the church assumes will come about as a consequence of its own existence.

Indirect action which the church strives to bring about is, again, of two types. It is always, of course, action by individual Christians, but the church's attitude toward this action may take the form of educating the consciences of its members or of acting as a home base for active cell groups committed to one or another social reform for the benefit of society.

From very early in his career Bennett has stressed the primary value of indirect action which takes the form of educating the conscience of the laity. The most effective social functioning of the church, he argued in 1938 (with a reference to Oldham), comes "not through its official agencies, not even through its clergy, but through its lay membership in the course of their work in the world. . . . What the minister proclaims as an independent prophet has less effect than what the laymen in his Church do."[9] The church must contribute to the laity a vision, standards, and a habit of self-criticism against which the social order can be measured.

Again, five years later, the most important thing that the church does is not the passing of resolutions and the publication of pamphlets, but "what the members of the Church do in their respective vocations in the world . . . as molders of public opinion." The local church is supremely important as an agency to encourage Christians to purge their motivations of self-interest and to identify with the interests of the underprivileged.[10] The minister must understand that, "the most important decisions in any community will be made by laymen. . . ."[11]

Thus, for Bennett, the basic social function of the church is

[9] Bennett, "New Emphases in Christian Social Teaching" (1938), p. 532.
[10] Bennett, "Enduring Bases" (1943), p. 29.
[11] Bennett, "Inaugural Address" (1943), p. 6.

educational. He could agree with F. Ernest Johnson that social education is "the prime responsibility of the Church."[12] Johnson had argued that there must be an "adequate demarcation of function" between the church and secular institutions.[13] The function of the church was to concern itself with spiritual and moral values. This would not so much limit its range of concern as it would dictate the kinds of things that the church should do to implement them. Since its primary concern is education, the church should not, for instance, maintain an independent system of welfare agencies which would compete with those of the state. Instead the church should cooperate with the secular welfare workers by acting as a moral teacher.[14]

Bennett's word for the content of Christian education is, of course, the Christian perspective. This was important as the basis for social action:

... at the present time there are so many groups, even within what has been called Christendom, which flatly deny fundamental Christian assumptions. If you can take the more conventional Christian assumptions for granted you have something to build on, the importance of which is evident only when those assumptions are absent.[15]

Racial discrimination, for example, is more easily combated within a moral context which undermines it than elsewhere.

By 1941 Bennett was arguing that we must recognize that the end of the spiritual and moral unity of the West, based on Christian and humanist assumptions, was at hand. The realization of this fact suggested that "even watered-down Christianity had an important function in the community and that at least it preserved an environment within which a more prophetic Christianity could be given a hearing."[16]

[12] F. Ernest Johnson, *The Church and Society* (1935), p. 222.
[13] *Ibid.*, p. 204.
[14] *Ibid.*, pp. 143–165.
[15] Bennett, "New Emphases in Christian Social Teaching" (1938), p. 534.
[16] *CR*, pp. 2–3.

Bennett has consistently held that the importance of the acknowledgment of certain moral principles by society is hard to exaggerate. These principles constitute a kind of ethos which maintains behavior on a fairly high plane. A vital religious and moral ethos can produce "a vast amount of decency and heroism."[17] But after the war Bennett was less sure that this ethos had been destroyed. In *Christian Ethics and Social Policy* he claimed that "there is still an impressive deposit of Christian moral convictions in most secular nations that have had a Christian background."[18] A self-consciously Christian civilization was not, he thought, to be expected, but the formation of a Christian ethos was desirable:

It is something to be thankful for when we do find great communities still able to recognize that Christian ethics has a claim upon them and still wistfully and with faith or half-believingly keeping their children under the influence of the Church.[19]

The fact that Christianity has lost influence on this level of unconsciously accepted assumptions has weakened our society.[20] The long term influence of the church which nurtures the conscience of the community is basic to all other action it may take. Once the "spirit and ethos, the moral sensitivities, and the value systems of the community" have been effected social change is much more practicable.[21]

Consequently, the primary objective of the Church's indirect

[17] Bennett, Book Review of Pitirim A. Sorokin, *Man and Society in Calamity* in *Religion in Life*, No. 12 (1943), p. 457. Bennett's remark is prompted by a table Sorokin includes which shows that faced with starvation only 1% of the population turn to cannibalism. Most people help their fellows. Bennett observed: "Here we see the enormous power of the moral and religious ethos in a society."

[18] *CESP*, p. 99.

[19] Bennett, "Forms of Ecumenical Christianity" (1946), p. 75.

[20] Bennett, "Amsterdam and the Social Crisis" (1948), p. 570.

[21] *CS*, pp. 278–279; cf. F. Ernest Johnson, *op. cit.*, p. 142, "The Church is, potentially, a culture-center for motive and conviction upon which the nation may depend for a spiritual undergirding of its social programs."

113

action is the promulgation of the Christian perspective. In his first book Bennett argued that the most important thing for the church to do was ". . . the teaching and preaching of the basic ethical and religious principles which are relevant to the social problem" and: "If this is neglected the Church might as well leave the rest of its social strategy to other agencies."[22] Yet the church had to do more than this. Education could not deal only with generalities:

> The preaching of general goals . . . will get its sharpness and become more than a series of platitudes if it is linked with the most specific statement possible about present evils. . . . the best way to make . . . repentance real is not to begin by blaming people but rather so to expose the evils related to their lives that they come to blame themselves and come to feel that moral restlessness in the face of evil which is beyond their control which is akin to repentance.[23]

Education is not to be confined to defense of the perspective, but is to go on to answer the questions about its consequences. The church's directives to its members may be more specific than simple exhortations to be loving. As it tries to raise the moral tone of the community as a whole, the church can teach its members, "what the Christian faith means in relation to economic justice and human unity." The church may go on to define Christian standards by which existing institutions and all programs for their alteration should be criticized. Its criticisms should be very concrete.[24]

The church must teach its members about the "meaning of Christian faith for the great public issues of the time" which means about the "goals and criteria which should influence decisions." In Bennett's view this involves showing "the human consequences of what is being done and of what may be proposed."[25] Thus the indirect influence of the church through its

[22] SS, p. 122.
[23] SS, p. 122.
[24] Cf. CESP, pp. 104–108 and chapter 6 below.
[25] CS, pp. 280–281.

114

membership acting in their various social roles is not at all a vague influence. This indirect influence involves direct teaching about social goals and standards. The *indirection* comes at the level of application. It is not the church as a corporation which enacts the teaching.

A significant amount of Professor Bennett's professional attention has been devoted to the question of just how specific the church can be in providing guidance for its members. This question will be taken up below, in chapter 6. At this point what is to be noticed is that this guidance to the membership is a form of indirect action by the church, and that it is the most important form of the church's social action. Socially the church is primarily an educational institution.[26]

Secondly, Bennett holds, the church takes intentional but indirect action through the fostering of cell groups. The church can help its members to act through the sponsorship of semi-official and voluntary groups of diverse kinds: those who share a common job, those with similar political convictions, or those whose political convictions differ. In sponsoring these groups the church should make clear that the views of their members do not commit the church as a whole.[27]

These same points were advanced by J. H. Oldham in the essay already referred to. Oldham claimed that the indirect action of the church would be advanced by "the multiplication of small groups of Christians for the purpose of mutual help in Christian witness and action." The organizing principle might be political, geographical, or professional. The important thing to note was that:

Wherever there has been a revival of Christianity of an enduring kind it has generally found expression in the spontaneous activity of small groups meeting for mutual encouragement, fellowship and common effort. The conception of "cells" is wholly congruous with

[26] Of course there is good reason to think that the New Testament better supports an alternative view, namely, that the primary role of the church is ministry or enactment, not education.

[27] *CS*, pp. 280–281.

the genius of Christianity. May not the formation of such cells of Christian witness and service be the distinctive Christian contribution to the social and political struggles of our time?[28]

Oldham's assertion of this point, that adventurous and prophetic groups were needed within the church, included a reference to F. Ernest Johnson's book *The Church and Society*.[29] Johnson had claimed that those who criticized the church for including people with sub-Christian conviction ignored the fact that the church draws its membership from people of all classes. Far from being a voluntary association dedicated to the social cause of a specific class, the church has a social function with respect to all of society. That function is, as was mentioned above, one primarily of education.

Yet Johnson thought there was a place within the church for groups which try to stand for a more radical social ideal than that which society as a whole is ready to acknowledge. Protestantism should follow the example of Roman Catholicism's policy of "incorporating the sects into her own life."[30] Movements such as the Methodist Federation for Social Service and the (Episcopal) Church League for Industrial Democracy "*belong within* the Church, but they can not be identified with it without falsification."[31]

Johnson's method of resolving the question of whether the church should be a "church" or a "sect" was to say that it should be a "church" which included "sects." Against radical critics of the church he vigorously defended the church's responsibility to the whole society whose spiritual aide it represented. Yet the more radical groups represented a kind of higher righteousness. Johnson compared his distinction between the church as a whole and the role of activistic groups within it to Calvin's distinction between the visible and the invisible

[28] Oldham, "The Function of the Church in Society," p. 198.
[29] *Ibid.*, pp. 229–230.
[30] Johnson, *op. cit.*, p. 82.
[31] *Ibid.*, p. 77.

church[32] and concluded that part of the function of minority pressure within the church was:

. . . to lift the level of the whole body and to make it more sensitive and more responsive to the finer implications of the Christian gospel. As it succeeds in this task the whole body of the Church moves to a more truly Christian position.[33]

This way of preserving the strengths of an inclusive church and the vigor of an exclusive fellowship has been a constant leitmotif in Bennett's writing. In 1935 he argued against the formation of radical religious movements apart from the church on the grounds that such one-sided movements would probably forget the "ultimate human problems which are common to every age and every social order." Such separate radical groups would only further divide the already fragmented resources of Christianity; and would "lose contact with the very constituency which needs to be leavened by a radical social vision."[34]

Yet within the same year he argued, in *Social Salvation,* that the church should encourage:

. . . the formation of groups which will commit themselves to more positive social programs. . . . the members of these movements will still represent the Church to some degree, but when they act or speak they will do so as individual Christians, as far as possible, rather than as Churchmen.[35]

As examples of the sort of group he had in mind Bennett listed the Fellowship of Reconciliation and the Fellowship of Socialist Christians. Just how vital the Christian social message was, he said, could be seen by the number of Christians allying themselves with movements like this. Action of this kind was very important if the church was not to be confronted with a situation of having to choose among choices shaped without reference to Christian ideals.

[32] *Ibid.,* pp. 87–88.
[33] *Ibid.,* pp. 91–92.
[34] Bennett, "The World Needs the Church" (1935), p. 31.
[35] *SS,* pp. 128–129.

Subsequently, in *Christian Realism,* Bennett still affirmed that the churches should give maximum encouragement to "pioneering groups which, driven by their Christian faith, work for a more Christian society through particular movements and programs."[36] Later, in *Christian Ethics and Social Policy,* he claimed that the church should serve as a laboratory "where it is possible to push further in the realization of Christian goals for human life than can be done in society at large."[37] The cell groups could not claim that they represented the whole church, but the church should claim that it included groups which were willing to dedicate themselves to Christianity in the face of a hostile world. By fostering these groups the church acted on society in an indirect way.

At this point one must admit that a problem is hidden under Bennett's distinction between direct and indirect action by the church. For Bennett action by church members in conformity with social principles taught by the church is "indirect" action by the church. While this is consistent with some of Bennett's remarks about the clergy, it is very unfortunate because it suggests that the layman in his vocation is somehow less the church than a member of the ecclesiastical bureaucracy making a pronouncement. Thus the distinction is theologically misleading. Further, it is politically unfortunate because it obscures the fact that through this individual in society the corporate church is affecting society in a very definite way. If, for instance, a particular form of economic organization is virtually anathematized by the church and church members consequently vote against candidates who espouse that form of organization, then the *church* has acted socially. I do not mean to deny the value of Bennett's distinctions between various forms of commitment on the part of the church. What must be noticed is that what he calls "indirect" church action is in part action by the community of Christians with the self-conscious purpose of bringing about certain social changes.

[36] *CR*, p. 152.
[37] *CESP*, p. 70.

Another *kind* of indirect action by the church is a result of its very existence as a social unit. This type of action is not so much intentional action by the church as it is a consequence or effect of the church's life as one society among others. In principle it is not at all inconceivable that other social bodies have these same effects in greater or lesser degree.

The first effect of this kind that the church has is the counteraction of totalitarianism. The church is a discrete social entity and it resists being swallowed up within some other and supposedly superior social unit. Consequently, as it seeks to be itself it finds itself essentially opposed to a certain kind of social organization. Its success in this struggle is to the benefit of all those who also oppose the totalitarian state.

That the church's life yields this indirect social effect has been one of Bennett's constant themes. As early as *Social Salvation* he claimed that the mere existence of the church was an obstacle to the "complete regimentation of life because the Church by its very nature claims a degree of spiritual freedom which cannot tolerate the totalitarian state." At that time the reason given for this claim was the transcendent character of Christian sanctions and loyalties.[38] By 1941 the rationale had taken a more characteristic form. The church is not, Bennett said in *Christian Realism,* "free to be the Church in all environments,"[39] which meant that she must set herself in opposition to certain political movements.

The existence of a community with "a faith and commission which transcend the perspective of the nation" is of "incalculable" value within the nation.[40] The church will always oppose totalitarianism because it is "the bearer of a tradition that is different from any national tradition and from any new ideology that may become the official doctrine of any state."[41]

The fact that American Christians live not just within the

[38] *SS,* p. 110.
[39] *CR,* p. 83.
[40] *CESP,* pp. 102–103.
[41] *CCT* (1948–62), p. 131.

national community but within the world Christian community as well is "the chief root of our best freedom."[42]

Further, the international character of the church is the source of a second unintentional indirect effect. The church is a forum for world reconciliation. Because it is an international fellowship it protects against international war. "It alone is able to speak to the world in the name of an authority which overarches the authority of nations." In 1935 that authority was enhanced because the church was making "the necessary frontal attack on the war system."[43]

After the Second World War, if the nations were patient, they could be sure that "it is in the Church that reconciliation between the peoples can begin." The church provided a "bridge" over the "breach within humanity" opened by that war. It was "one strand of community among the nations which already exists and which can be a major support for the necessary international political institutions."[44] The international fellowship of the church provided it with a perspective "from which it will be possible to control the tendencies toward hatred and vengeance."[45]

Once the war was over it was clear that the church could act "as a bond that unites men, in spite of particular conflicts between them." What the church could do along these lines was limited by the racial and social divisions within the church and by the church's admittedly finite outreach—it could, for example, do nothing to reconcile a conflict between Moslems and Hindus. Nevertheless the church's potential for good along these lines was strikingly suggested by "examples of solidarity among Christians of the world during the period of the war and its immediate aftermath."[46]

[42] Bennett, "How My Mind Has Changed" (1959), p. 1502.
[43] SS, p. 114.
[44] Bennett, "The Christian Basis for Enduring Peace" (1944), p. 751.
[45] Bennett, "The Protestant Churches and World Order," *World Order: Its Intellectual and Cultural Foundations,* ed. F. Ernest Johnson (New York, 1945), pp. 127–128.
[46] CESP, p. 100.

More recently the point remains the same. Simply by being its unitary self and with no political purpose in view, the church maintains an international fellowship which aids in the reconciliation of the nations.[47] The formal relationships between states do not supplant personal relations. These personal, human, relations are maintained by other international associations such as those of scientists and civil servants, but "as a theologian" Bennett is concerned to emphasize the role of the international church. When these personal ties are maintained it is harder to go to war.[48]

Thus not only is it the case that the consensus of the ecumenical church has great weight for the Christian conscience, it is also true that the international church has an important social status. In an early article Bennett claimed that the most potent historical forces were not military and political but spiritual. They were the forces suggested to Christians by the Cross and Resurrection. There was a bigger job than checking the force of military action:

. . . the job of keeping alive moral sensitivity, of keeping alive the recognition of our own sins and of divine judgement upon them; it is the job of caring for the victims of war and persecution . . . [etc.] Already in the world Church we have a structure which is favorable to this constructive emphasis.[49]

Again, in *Christian Realism*, ". . . the only strand of world community that shows any signs of holding is the Christian Church." Therefore: "As a bond between persons that moderate class conflict, and as a critic of all centers of power the Church has an indispensable function."[50] Which meant that, at least for Christians:

[47] *CS*, pp. 279–280.
[48] Bennett, "Moral Tensions in International Affairs," a pamphlet published by The Council on Religion and International Affairs, 1964, pp. 13–14.
[49] Bennett, "The Christian's Ethical Decision" (1940), p. 399.
[50] *CR*, pp. 138f.

121

. . . the strengthening of the world Church is more important than anything we may feel called upon to do on the political level, for we know that by this means we will preserve and perhaps increase resources for the new world that must come as men are driven . . . to seek ways of organizing their common life which are closer to the intention of God.[51]

In *Christian Ethics and Social Policy* Bennett argued that the existence of the Christian church had the ethical significance for the Christian of making him a citizen of two cities. And:

The Christian Church, with all its shortcomings, is the only school in which we are trained for this dual citizenship. . . . The Church is the one association which has proved over and over again to be so tough that the state cannot absorb it.[52]

Membership in the world church gives a man another loyalty besides his loyalty to his nation or state. It makes a man a part of an international fellowship. While the church is not absolutely unique in this regard (since various other international organizations have the same effect), the implication remains clear that in fact the church is the most important international brotherhood. The ecumenical Christian community has been "more effective in overcoming purely national barriers than any other."[53] It is particularly effective in countering totalitarianism and nationalism because it consists of a socially heterogeneous membership and lives in response to a socially transcendent God.

Thus the church has significant indirect effects both internationally and intra-nationally. Because the church is a group

---

[51] *CR*, pp. 158–159.

[52] *CESP*, pp. 90–91; cf. p. 87: "The fact that I am at the same time both a citizen of a nation and the member of a universal Church is a source of considerable ethical freedom. . . . In the case of many decisions that limit our action, decisions that mean taking sides for one movement or party against another, membership in the Church furnishes a relationship across the line of conflict that may modify the conflict itself." Cf. Bennett, Editorial: "The Christian's Dual Citizenship" in *Christianity and Crisis*, V, No. 5 (April 2, 1945), p. 1.

[53] *CS*, p. 187.

organized with reference to a supranational object, it counteracts the tendencies of a national community to claim the total allegiance of its constituents or claim that it is exclusively able to define legitimate social relationships. The church's existence keeps the state from being internally total and externally total. These actions or effects of the church are "indirect" in the sense that Christian loyalty is not to the church but to "that which it represents."[54] Any organization existing for supranational purposes would have these effects to a greater or lesser extent.

The indirect social action of the church, then, is of two very different kinds. On the one hand, the church engages in social education and the sponsorship of cell groups with the objective of making both the fundamental conceptions on which we base our judgments and our actual political ethos more Christian. On the other hand, the church as an international society creates a loyalty which effectively inhibits the totalitarian and irreconcilable passions of nationalism. What these kinds of social action have in common is that they do not represent a direct social action by the church itself. The agent involved is either an individual Christian or the church as one among many supranational social bodies.

Yet the church must also take direct social action. Direct action is "actually of less importance than the Church's indirect witness and action."[55] Not only is it less effective, it is dangerous. Direct political action by the church runs the risk of mixing the potent passions of religion and politics.[56] Furthermore, from the church's point of view, its responsibility is not primarily the restraint of a social evil such as Communism but the presentation of "its faith by word and life to the people of all conditions and lands, that they may find for themselves the essential truth about life."[57]

---

[54] Bennett, "Moral Tensions" (1964), pp. 13–14.
[55] Bennett, "Forms of Ecumenical Christianity" (1946), p. 77.
[56] See, for example, *WCMPD,* p. 14.
[57] *CCT* (1948–62), p. 186.

Nevertheless, the church must not stop with indirect action. If it is effective in indirect action, direct action will be expected. Times will come when ". . . it will be necessary for the Church to find ways in which . . . its word can be spoken to the world and it can be counted on one side or the other."[58] "There will sometimes arise situations," Bennett wrote in *Social Salvation*, "in which it is hard to believe that the Church should be neutral when political choices are being made." For example bills to abolish child labor, provide for a public lottery (!) or a bigger navy cannot meet a neutral response by the church. The kind of action then recommended consists of teaching that politics must be morally responsible, clarifying the issues as they appear from the Christian perspective, and, yet, forming no allegiance with a particular political party.[59]

The church must be willing to take direct political action. It can not stand aloof from the question of how the ideals it proclaims fare in history. Social and political movements must be used by the church "because it is through partisan politics that social decisions are made."[60] Direct forms of action are "far less important," "more precariously based" and should be "less frequent" than indirect action, but a constituency aroused by indirect action will demand that "the Churches take additional steps intended to influence public policy more directly."[61] Furthermore, ". . . if the Churches never act or speak directly this is likely to be a sign not of restraint, but of their not caring enough."[62]

The basic form of direct action by the church is a statement on the issue involved produced by a particular body of churchmen. It consists of ". . . the arrangement officially by the Churches of processes which enable a responsible group to

[58] Bennett, "Forms of Ecumenical Christianity" (1946), p. 77.
[59] *SS*, pp. 126–128.
[60] Bennett, "Exponent of Social Christianity," *This Ministry: The Contribution of Henry Sloane Coffin*, ed. Reinhold Niebuhr (New York, 1945), pp. 87–88.
[61] *CS*, p. 281.
[62] *CS*, p. 284.

speak for itself to the Church or to the community." This is the system adopted by both the World and National Councils of Churches. The statements produced in this way have great "intrinsic authority."[63]

These pronouncements are indirect action insofar as they can be considered education of individual church members. But, as Bennett says, "Such guidance may be overheard by the public."[64] The churches not only guide their own members. "They also attempt to give guidance to the electorate and to the government." The distinction between these two forms of action becomes very difficult to maintain in the case of supposedly intra-Church teaching that appears in the public forum. Bennett likes to refer in this connection to a letter by the Presbyterian Church against the McCarthy panic which was published in full in *The New York Times*. He approves of the publication of the letter and of this kind of action in general, if it has a competent basis in the churches. Such action "can do much to bring a Christian judgment to bear upon public affairs."[65] Reports of various commissions and conferences are addressed to the constituencies of the churches "rather than *for* the Churches *to* the world; but it is expected that the world will overhear." The authority of these statements is not ecclesiastical, but grows out of "the confidence that Churches have in the insight of those who formulate them."[66]

The relationship between statements of various conferences and commissions and the church as a whole represents a delicate spot in Professor Bennett's thought. In the 1930's, when his fundamental objective was to show that the church as such could and did act socially, he suggested that its leadership could act for it. Thus, ". . . when we raise the question as to what part the Church should take in the economic struggle, we

---

[63] *CS*, pp. 282–283.
[64] *WCMPD*, p. 112.
[65] *CS*, pp. 281–282.
[66] Bennett, "Results of an Ecumenical Study" in *Christendom*, IX (1944), p. 152.

are thinking of what part its articulate leadership should take."
Action by articulate and informed church members was action
by the church:

> When this articulate membership acts and speaks, it may not do
> so officially but it does in fact represent the Church. Any minister
> or professor or board secretary who uses time paid for by the
> Church, or who uses his strategic place in the Church to bring
> the membership at large to an acceptance of his conception of the
> Christian task is in a peculiar sense the Church in action.[67]

By the 1940's however, Bennett was less sure that church
officials could be said to represent the church. One had to distinguish the resolutions of official church bodies from the activities of church-sponsored agencies. These in turn were different
from statements made in sermons, from positions taken by
ministers and church officials as citizens, and from the stands
of various unofficial groups of ministers and laymen. "There is
a wide range here in the extent to which the Church as such
is committed."[68]

In other words, one must "distinguish between the various
degrees of authoritativeness in corporate action by the Church."
The most authoritative commitment a church could make
would be the incorporation "of support of a specific social
policy into the creed or ethos of the Church" (this has in effect
been done with respect to pacifism by the Quakers). The next
most authoritative form of commitment is "the resolutions of
the representative Church bodies" such as the Presbyterian
General Assembly. Less authoritative and hard to rank are the
actions taken by leaders who can not be dissociated from the
church, policies of church boards, and action by the executive
committee of the (then) Federal Council of Churches ("which
in theory speaks for itself but which also appears to speak for
the whole constituency to some extent").

[67] *SS*, p. 117.
[68] Bennett, "Enduring Bases" (1943), pp. 28–29.

Thus an agency like the Congregational Council for Social Action's Legislative Service does not commit the church, whereas a Presbyterian (U.S.A.) report on industrial relations, adopted as its official position by the General Assembly in 1944 (which *almost* required joining a labor union) came much closer to being church action. The Congregational agency does not commit the church as church; the Presbyterian action was an official position.[69]

Once it is clear that not everything that a Christian leader says commits the church to the same extent, however, Bennett wants it made very clear that churchmen must speak up. They should observe necessary tentativeness, be aware of the finitude of their judgment and of the right of others to disagree. Then, they should "speak or act without serious inhibitions." He quotes R. H. Tawney: "When to speak is unpopular, it is less pardonable to be silent than to say too much."[70]

Bennett freely admits that the churches sometimes speak too casually and that sometimes it would be better for them to be silent. A worthwhile pronouncement must be the product of a "carefully organized process of consultation."[71] Nevertheless Bennett thinks the church should greatly increase the amount of guidance given to its members. Many fear social guidance by the church:

. . . because they do not want to have even the most indirect association with statements with which they do not fully agree. They prefer to have the Church remain silent until it can speak officially with decisive authority. There are others, and I am one of them, who fear that if the Church is so restrained it will seldom say anything that is important until it is too late. What is needed is as much corporate Christian guidance as possible. The emphasis should be placed on its intrinsic rather than its official authority, and freedom to oppose it must be taken for granted.[72]

[69] *CESP*, pp. 108–113.
[70] Bennett, "Enduring Bases" (1943), pp. 28–29.
[71] *CS*, p. 283.
[72] *CESP*, p. 111.

127

It may be illuminating to compare this view with some remarks by J. H. Oldman in the essay already mentioned. Oldham argued that the church should make pronouncements which would either serve as a support for the views of the individual minister or influence the decisions of government officials. But, he went on, these pronouncements would have no effect if they did not actually represent the opinions of "those whose opinions they profess to represent." One must be very clear about who is committed by a given pronouncement. Furthermore:

It is surprising how often the sense of responsibility may be lacking in Christian assemblies. The danger is perhaps greatest in inter-denominational and international bodies, in which sometimes resolutions are passed as an expression of the Christian mind on a particular public issue, when they do not in fact represent more than the opinions of the more or less chance collection of individuals who happen to be present at the meeting.[73]

Oldham tried to guard against some of these dangers in his organization of the Oxford Conference of 1937. He meant to restrain the making of pronouncements not only by insisting that the church know all the facts before it speak but, further, by insisting that as a necessary step of preparation it submit "these facts and the conclusions drawn from them to those who have to deal in a practical capacity with the questions involved."[74] Evidently Bennett means to agree with his views about the authority of pronouncements, but to push for more frequent use of the technique.

How specific may the pronouncements of the church be?

[73] Oldham, "The Function of the Church in Society," pp. 223–224; cf. Johnson, op. cit., who holds that church pronouncements are often not "really expressive of more than minority opinion" (p. 86) and that, while the promulgation of social creeds is within the competence of the church, ". . . when the Church speaks and acts in relation to social issues it should be reflecting a corporate conviction and not a minority opinion that has little significance for the group as a whole" (p. 140).
[74] Ibid., p. 222.

Bennett's answer to this question is basically the same as that of William Temple. Temple held that the church's essential commitment was to "the everlasting Gospel and to the creeds which formulate it" rather than to "an ephemeral program of detailed action."[75] Therefore the church should not support a particular policy. Nevertheless as a morally committed group, the church should "announce Christian principles and point out where the existing social order at any time is in conflict with them."[76] The positive affirmations of the church could not be said to entail a given policy, but they did show what was wrong with certain policies or conditions. There was nothing wrong with the church observing that something was un-christian.

Similarly, for Bennett, the church may state the contradiction between a certain political action and Christian social teaching. Not only is it to teach its members definite social principles, it also need not stand mute when it sees these principles violated. For example, Bennett approves of the declaration of the Roman Catholic Archbishop who reacted to the nomination of Lester Maddox by announcing: "No honest Catholic can vote

[75] William Temple, *Christianity and Social Order*, pp. 27–29.

[76] *Ibid.*, p. 50; for Temple's principles see pp. 50–74. Also see pp. 30–32. For Temple the church's statement of principles should "carry with it a denunciation of customs or institutions in contemporary life and practice which offend against those principles." Yet Temple had a clear sense of the limitation of the church's competence in this regard: "These principles [of Christian living] and their order of subordination the Church should know and proclaim; and the Christian citizen should take his part in the political arena, striving to conform the practice of his country to them. But the responsibility for judging what is prac-ticable at any given moment in this sinful world belongs to statesmen and politicians, and not to ecclesiastics as such; for, as a wise man has put it, 'It is the duty of Lambeth to remind Westminster that Westminster is responsible to God; but this does not mean that Westminster is re-sponsible to Lambeth' " (*Malvern, 1941*, p. 15). It has been some time since Bennett referred to this quotation (Editorial: "William Temple" in *Christianity and Crisis*, II, No. 9 [June 1, 1942], pp. 1–2). Cf. also Eduard Heimann, *Freedom and Order*, p. 218; this whole procedure is the one mapped out at the Oxford Conference (cf. Oldham [ed.], *Oxford Conference: Official Report*, pp. 98–104).

129

for a segregationist." According to Bennett the Archbishop was simply stating a matter of fact: "the contradiction between Catholic teaching and segregation."[77]

Rigorous and precise criticism of the existing situation is "an essential part of the prophetic function of the Church." Precision is the surest way "of preventing general principles from becoming harmless platitudes." Therefore the church should develop expertise on the human consequences of policies.[78] Against someone who holds that the church should confine itself to the level of the perspective, Bennett wonders "what are the Churches to do when they have observed the effects of wrong or dubious perspectives in the actual performance of policy-makers?" Even if the churches can not suggest an alternative, the legitimacy of their concern with perspectives implies "that they should be able to cry out against the end-product of the perspectives that they have criticized."[79]

However, the church can do more than make judgments of this sort. It can bring the consensus to which it has arrived, "to the attention of the agencies of government," that is, its leaders may testify before legislative committees, letters to the president may be written and so forth.[80] Most typically this kind of action by the church begins by the church knowing "with clarity what it is against."[81] Given a radical situation of the sort created by a candidate for public office who openly champions white supremacy, very specific political guidance to the membership of the churches may be in order.[82]

[77] Bennett, "Authority in Christian Social Ethics" (1967), pp. 15–16; Bennett says that he wishes the Archbishop had said "no consistent Catholic can vote for a segregationist" since that would have left the question of honesty to the confessional.

[78] CC, p. 37.

[79] Bennett, FPCP, p. 157. This is a response to R. Paul Ramsey in Christianity and Crisis, XXV, No. 11 (June 28, 1965).

[80] CS, pp. 283–284.

[81] CESP, p. 114.

[82] Bennett, "The Religious Concern With Politics," published by the National Conference of Christians and Jews (1963), p. 17; for instances of Bennett's moving in this direction see Editorial: "The Candidacy of Mr. Nixon" in Christianity and Crisis, XIX, No. 24 (January 25, 1960),

In no case should Christians form a Christian political party. Movements supporting political and economic programs represent "a great mixture of human motives." Thus loyalty to movements of this kind must be secondary and under constant Christian criticism.[83] Although the churches might at times unite to oppose a political party (for example, one dedicated to white supremacy):

Christian political parties and Christian political movements in general misrepresent the true situation: they give the impression that Christianity implies a particular political program whereas it does not do so.[84]

Religious parties are to be avoided, "at all cost."[85] He is in agreement with the Amsterdam Assembly (section III) in holding that they may be necessary at some times and places, but they create a problem in that the more successful they are the more surely they become "vested interest[s] which create religious confusion."[86] It is one thing to try to influence legislation and legislators; it is another to make the church one of the many participants in the political process. Even when a given particular candidate must be opposed this remains true:

. . . let us make it unmistakeably clear that the Church is not a political society, that there is no Christian political party, that no one should be excommunicated because of his political opinions.[87]

---

pp. 209–210 (cf. *Christianity and Crisis*, XX, No. 4 (March 21, 1960), pp. 31–32) and editorial: "The Goldwater Nomination" in *Christianity and Crisis*, XXIV, No. 14 (August 3, 1964), p. 157.

[83] Bennett, "Enduring Bases" (1943), p. 26.

[84] *CS*, pp. 288–289; but cf. Bennett's attitude toward the Republican Party in "Focus for Christian Action" in *Christianity and Society*, XVIII, No. 4 (Fall, 1953), p. 20.

[85] Bennett, "The Religious Concern with Politics" (1963), p. 18.

[86] *WCMPD*, p. 115; cf. World Council of Churches, *The First Assembly of the World Council of Churches*, pp. 80–82.

[87] Bennett, "God and Caesar," an unpublished pre-election sermon (1964), pp. 7–8.

131

Thus Professor Bennett has given much attention to the question of what the church should and should not do. The church may indirectly act for the welfare of men in various ways: it may educate its members, stimulate their social analysis or action, and act as one of the several supranational social bodies which combat the invidious national and international effects of loyalty to the nation state. On the other hand, it may directly act by enunciating principles, criticizing policies, and attempting to influence legislation. It should not form a political party, for such an allegiance would force it to sacrifice its true character.

The question of what, in Professor Bennett's view, the church ought to stand for we will consider now.

6. CHRISTIAN SOCIAL PRINCIPLES AND "MIDDLE AXIOMS"

What, according to Bennett, does the consensus of the ecumenical church stand for? He could probably agree with William Temple that "Freedom is the goal of politics. To establish a secure true freedom is the primary object of all right political action."[1] Freedom, or liberty (Bennett does not systematically distinguish them) is the highest social value. In politics it is of the utmost importance that liberty "not be sacrificed to equality." And the reason for this is: "If we drive ahead with only the concern for equality we shall lose quality. We shall lose the liberty to be different." Similarly, in economics, a "single-track" concentration on equality would reduce incentive, cause regimentation, and make difficult the existence of independent social institutions which are favorable to freedom.[2]

The sources of our understanding of what freedom is are diverse and it is undeniable that the social experience of recent generations has affected our understanding of what freedom should entail.[3] Nevertheless, the basic value of freedom has remained constant. As men grow and attempt to formulate their view of the world, they require freedom. Their welfare requires it. The need to decide for one's self is so basic that, as was pointed out above, even God does not deny it:

---

[1] Temple, *Christianity and Social Order*, p. 61.

[2] *CS*, pp. 160–161; cf. Bennett, "Freedom and Justice" (1959), pp. 331–332.

[3] Bennett, "Freedom and Justice" (1959), p. 324.

133

The risks of freedom, of the freedom to be wrong, the importance of enabling persons to come to see the truth for themselves, from their own insight—these belong to God's way of dealing with men.

God does not overwhelm men's minds. He wants men to find their true welfare sincerely. Therefore, on a social plane,

. . . when men coerce the minds of other men through false inducements or through playing upon fears, they sin against love, for they tempt their neighbors to be hypocrites.[4]

The freedom so necessary for human welfare has two important dimensions. First, the individual must have the right to be true to his own convictions. Second, and partly as a means to that end, the social strength of non-political associations such as the family and the university "which have norms that are independent of the state and of the contemporary majority" must be preserved. Finally, perhaps as another aspect of this last point: "Above all we must emphasize the freedom of the Church to be true to its own foundation in God's revelation in Christ, to be independent of control by the state and of domination by the national culture."[5]

The freedom of the church is a way of preserving freedom within the national society. For Bennett freedom is nothing if it does not suggest the independence of the individual against the national community. Collectivism is to be repudiated. Not only is the individual's conscience not to be coerced,[6] but also his physical welfare is to be provided for by society. Societies are judged by the extent to which they care for "marginal persons who do not seem to count or who are regarded as

---

[4] *Ibid.*, p. 327.

[5] *Ibid.*, p. 332. "Social fellowship" was the second of Temple's derivative principles. Freedom only became actual in such lesser associations, Temple held. A free society must be rich in subordinate fellowships. (*Christianity and Social Order*, pp. 64–69.)

[6] *CCT* (1948–62), p. 51; Bennett likes to refer to Luther's treatise on *Secular Authority* in this connection; cf. *CS*, pp. 136–137.

offenders against society, as political obstacles, or as national enemies."[7]

Therefore, in Bennett's terms it is ludicrous to suggest that a society is free if it simply allows the strong to victimize the weak. The freedom of all members of society is of value. No ideology should suggest that a man's freedom to exist is trivial. Failure to recognize this is a great failure of the Communist political ideology. There is no check on the tendency to treat certain individuals simply as obstacles to be removed. Communism has a tendency to lose interest in the dignity and freedom of the person.

Such a loss of interest is impossible for Christianity which knows that the individual is the unit of religious decision, that the faithful perspective on reality includes an affirmation about human existence, and that Jesus Christ was incarnate in an individual man. The Christian will naturally reject all social theories which "lead to a situation in which the person is a mere creature of the state."[8] When the Christian stands for freedom in society he always means at least that he stands for the freedom of the individual against society.

This is not to say that he stands for anarchy. Freedom requires order. For Bennett order is almost synonymous with peace. A society in which social relations are regulated and in which violence is minimized has order. If the people are not slitting one another's throats, there is order, although not necessarily a just order. Justice is a word which more accurately describes some orders than others.

Order, or peace, is necessary for human existence. It is a physical necessity of life. Bennett is very impressed with Eduard Heimann's discussion of the dialectic between order and freedom. Heimann argued that whereas freedom was more spiritually necessary than order, order was more physically necessary. Order was more fundamental; freedom was higher, because "what matters is freedom." The demands of order and

[7] Bennett, "Christian Ethics and Current Issues" (1965), pp. 7–8.
[8] CCT (1948–62), pp. 476 and 100–109.

freedom will never coincide. By definition a structure of social order must impose limitations on the freedom of the members of society. Freedom, for its part, means "a reservation exempted from the strictness of order."[9]

Thus, for Bennett, order is not of value for its own sake but as a means to freedom. He rejoices that it is no longer plausible to give theological sanction to the status quo. The old warnings against anarchy are not to be forgotten. We must remember that without social organization people would starve. He notices that it was the doctrine of sin that was used as a justification for sanctifying the existing order, but claims that this argument does not prove.

Christian teaching about sin is double-edged. It works against the temptations which accompany an order that is maintained by arbitrary power as well as against the dangers of anarchy. No order in the long run is tolerable, and in fact no order can endure, unless there is justice in it and unless it proves to be compatible with a considerable measure of human freedom.[10]

He admits that freedom would disappear without order, but claims that "if the order does not involve a strong trend toward economic justice, freedom itself becomes largely formal for the majority of men."[11] Order is a necessary but secondary social criterion. As suggested in the last quotations, a tolerable order must allow not only freedom; it must also be just. Man needs justice as well as freedom in his societies.

While the experiences of recent generations have transformed the concept of justice as well as that of freedom,[12] it is not at all obvious what *justice* means. The fact is that human

[9] Eduard Heimann, *Freedom and Order*, pp. 9–10; cf. Temple, *Christianity and Social Order*, p. 82: "Order is to be valued as the basis for freedom." "Freedom is a finer thing than order, but order is more indispensable than freedom."

[10] Bennett, "Christianity in its Political Setting" in *Religion in Life*, XXIV (1955), pp. 13–14.

[11] Bennett, "Freedom and Justice" (1959), p. 328.

[12] *Ibid.*, p. 324.

applications of the concept of justice differ "with differing conceptions of the rights of various segments of the community."[13] Therefore, it is necessary for the concept of justice to have an anchor. While the classic definition of justice is to give every man his due, what is due to people is variable. Love must suggest some content for it.

When one translates from the language of faith into the language of politics, the priority of faith is not compromised. What Bennett means to deny is that love is somehow superhuman, an unrealizable ideal to which the closest possible approximation is justice. That does not force him to deny that, on a human level, love is superior to justice, that, with respect to the question now at issue, the language of faith should determine the language of politics. When one translates from one language to another it is one's sentence in the first language that is controlling. With respect to love and justice, then,

The positive side of justice . . . is merely the translation of Christian love into terms that are relevant to social organization.[14]

On this basis the way to understand what "giving every man his due" means is to see that:

Justice on the positive side should be the organization of society in such a way as *to give every child his due.*[15]

When love is translated into a concept of justice, *justice* is transformed. Justice continues to mean the rejection of arbitrariness, an insistence that the social rules must be applied fairly. But it acquires a positive dimension which involves "the transformation of the rules themselves to meet the needs and to provide more favorable conditions for all people."[16] When

[13] *Ibid.,* p. 325.
[14] *CR,* p. 80.
[15] *CR,* p. 79; see below, n. 48.
[16] Bennett, "Christian Ethics and the National Conscience," p. 9.

137

the concept of justice becomes the vehicle for the demands of love it is "dynamic," "informed by imagination," and it "seeks to raise the neglected and exploited people."[17] Justice means concern for the welfare of the needy.

Bennett never says that only the Christian understands justice in this way. In fact, he certainly thinks that the transformed concept of justice in Western society is a function of, at least, Jewish as well as Christian influences.[18] But he does insist that it is socially important that there be people who will raise questions about the oppressed in a community. The moral sensitivity associated with love will affect the concept of justice maintained in a given community because "what the due of any person is depends upon a moral consensus in the community." Because Christians and others have been concerned with those in need no one today believes that slavery is due to someone, although that belief was held in the times of Aristotle and Aquinas.

Consequently when love transforms the concept of justice in a community it has an affect not only on the ideas that members of the community have, but on the actual possibilities for justice in that community. By transforming men's minds, love can transform their societies. If the consensus of what is due the oppressed has been leavened by Christianity in a given community, it will become easier for the economically exploited to receive their due share of the produce of their labor.[19]

All this suggests that there is a characteristic ingredient which love includes in a true understanding of justice. The Christian should stand for:

. . . a new interpretation of justice which is the result of the sensitive understandings of the equal claims of all children because of

[17] Bennett, "Freedom and Justice" (1959), p. 325.

[18] *WCMPD*, p. 103.

[19] Bennett, "Christian Ethics and Foreign Policy" in *Catholic Mind*, Vol. LX, No. 1161 (March, 1962), pp. 15–16. This was an address given October 27, 1961.

their special needs and of the recognition that in the case of children equality in rights overshadows all differences. It is justice transformed by love.[20]

The stress on need which one comes to expect is present, but there is another element: equality. Justice should include a large measure of equality. On its positive side justice means "that all persons and groups should be raised to the place where all have equal opportunity to develop their capacities and to make their characteristic contributions to the common life." This does not mean that we should pretend that all persons in all respects are equal. Nor does it mean (as mentioned before) that freedom is to be sacrificed to equality. It does mean that inequality embodied in social institutions must be rigorously criticized.[21]

Men are certainly not equal in all respects, but the Christian knows that all are equally objects of God's concern and, therefore, "in their claim upon the concern of all men who seek to be open to God's will for them." Second, the Christian knows that all men are sinful and in need of God's mercy. These fundamental similarities among men do not mean that society can know no inequalities but they "provide a basis for judgment" on all institutionalized inequalities.[22] They suggest, on the one hand, that all men regardless of race or class should have equal opportunity to be educated, to make a living, and so forth. This is the social correlate of the "positive side" of human nature discussed in chapter 1. On the other hand, despite the obvious need for functional hierarchies within society, every particular hierarchy should be kept under criticism because it will become pervaded by injustice. This is because all men are sinful.[23]

20 *CCT* (1948–62), pp. 137–138.
21 *CC*, pp. 31–32.
22 Bennett, "Freedom and Justice" (1959), p. 326. The stress on equality is clear as early as *CAOW*, p. 14.
23 *WCMPD*, pp. 22–23.

Unlike some of his contemporaries,[24] Bennett is unwilling to set up a kind of absolute hierarchy among the social values of freedom, order, justice, and equality. At this point he takes the inability of an individual human being to transcend a particular standpoint very seriously indeed. He does insist that the Christian community must translate the Christian perspective, and especially its main imperative, the command to love, into some such broad social criteria as these and that the objectives these criteria define are of continuing importance. They are essential ingredients in a society which will satisfy human needs, even if they are ingredients which may be combined in varying proportions.

Yet they are, undeniably, very general criteria. In order to be more meaningful they must be supplemented by more specific convictions. The name Bennett gives to these specific, supplementary propositions is "middle axioms." It is probable that this term is the one Bennett is most closely allied with in the eyes of most scholars. For that reason alone it is worthy of attention. At the same time it is a term which has often been misunderstood; therefore a recapitulation may be in order.

So far I have argued that for John Bennett the transition from statements of faith to political statements is not basically a transition from the abstractly true to that which is true in human life. It is not logical deduction, or a matter of the subsumption of particular cases. Rather that transition is made by translating the language of faith into the language of politics. The language of faith remains superior, in the sense that it is controlling, and the Christian faith is said to provide the best fundamental perspective. But the latter claim is made with respect to other faiths, and concepts of faith are not differentiated from those of politics by being more abstract.[25]

Yet Bennett's theory does include a description of the way

[24] For Heimann justice was the suprarational and therefore religious union of freedom and order (*op. cit.,* pp. 229–234). On Reinhold Niebuhr see above, chapter 2.
[25] See above chapter 3.

140

ethical reasoning moves from the general to the specific. There is a systematic way of making the transition from what is generally necessary (for instance, justice for the oppressed) to what a given person must do at a particular time (for instance, vote for fair housing legislation). This second transition takes place within the context of political language, after the translation is made. It is made by use of concepts of intermediate generality (in this case that justice requires anti-segregation legislation) which Bennett calls "middle axioms."

As will become evident, Bennett does refer to this second transition as a transition from more certainly Christian principles to those which are less certainly Christian. To understand this one must keep in mind that for Bennett the perspective includes only the most certainly Christian propositions. Political judgments obviously have less Christian warrant. But the way one gets from one to the other is complicated; it involves two shifts: the one described before—from the perspective to broad social criteria; and the one which will now be discussed—from broad social criteria to particular social judgments. Thus, looked at from a distance, the movement from the perspective to policy is the "movement" from the general to the specific, but on inspection it appears that the "movement" involves two "vectors": one horizontal, on a high level of generality (from perspective to criteria), the other vertical, from one degree of generality to another (from criteria to middle axioms). Although it must be admitted that Professor Bennett has not always made this clear, he has certainly acknowledged the distinction involved.[26] We must now discuss his formulation of the second movement.

One way of showing that for Bennett "middle axioms" are problematic because of their specificity, and not because of their epistemological foundation, is to see the origins of the concept in his thought. They come up under the rubric of "strategy" for the social action of the church. They are an

[26] Bennett, "Principles and the Context" (1961), p. 7.

attempt to answer the question of how specific the church should be.

In his first book, *Social Salvation,* Bennett discussed the problem of specific commitments by the church under the heading of the "social strategy" of the churches. He included as elements of the churches' social strategy, first, the dedication to general social goals, and, besides, "The support of definite next-steps apart from partisan politics and apart from specific legislation." These were to be "social objectives which are consistent with a variety of possible legislative measures embodying the details of method."[27] Examples of such objectives were the support of social insurance and the labor movement and the opposition to child labor. The following year, in *Christianity—And Our World,* Bennett made the same point, holding that in the social struggle for justice the church should stand for a few discriminate social objectives such as the freedom of economic groups to organize for self-protection.[28]

In 1937 Bennett went to England to aid in the preparations for the Oxford Conference. There he worked with Joseph H. Oldham whose influence on him has already been noticed. Oldham at that time was composing an essay on the function of the church in society. In it he argued that broad assertions or imperatives such as commands to love or to seek justice were not of much help to the conscience in particular cases. Yet he, as a self-styled defender of an ethic of inspiration, was anxious not to compromise the freedom of the individual in particular situations:

Hence between purely general statements of the ethical demands of the Gospel and the decisions that have to be made in concrete situations there is need for what may be described as middle axioms. It is these that give relevance and point to the Christian ethic. They are an attempt to define the direction in which, in a

[27] *SS,* pp. 125–126.
[28] *CAOW,* Chapter 3.

particular state of society, Christian faith must express itself. They are not binding for all time, but are provisional definitions of the type of behavior required of Christians at a given period and in given circumstances.[29]

This is the passage to which Bennett inevitably refers when he discusses middle axioms. Evidently Oldham understood himself to be arguing for the need for restrained definiteness in the expression of the church's social message.

Bennett did not immediately adopt the term "middle axiom." A book review published in 1937 uses what is in effect a synonym, "next steps."[30] Two statements from the late 1930's and early 1940's suggest the great influence of Reinhold Niebuhr on his thought about this question. We must be careful not to equate the Christian ideal with the "next best thing to be done," he argued in 1938, but that should not suggest to us the ideal's irrelevance. Instead it involves "the claim of the Christian ethic on us in every human relationship, with the recognition that in the relations between large-scale groups the principles by which we act are always in a state of tension with the Christian ideal."[31] Again, in *Christian Realism,* three years later, he urged the reader to recognize "that Christian love cannot be fully realized in a world of sin" but that "in most situations one political policy . . . is relatively more just than another." He explicitly says that he means to agree with Niebuhr here.[32]

Yet the structure of his own concerns was vividly present in that book. He discussed the problems of equating a given policy (he refers to pacifism) with God's will and concludes that "a more indirect relationship" between the Christian teaching and

[29] Oldham, "The Function of the Church in Society" (1937), pp. 209–210.
[30] Bennett, Review of Harry F. Laidler, *A Program for Modern America* in *Religion in Life,* VI (1937), p. 308.
[31] Bennett, "Christianity and Social Salvation" (1938), pp. 9–15.
[32] *CR*, pp. 96–98.

social issues must be formulated. The church should concentrate on teaching the Christian perspective. That perspective was to include such things as giving the benefit of the doubt to the underprivileged.[33] By 1943 he had adopted the phrase *middle axioms,* evidently using "specific goals" as a synonym.[34]

In the meantime another figure whose influence on Bennett has been noticed, William Temple, had associated himself with the middle axiom proposal. Christians, said Temple, know that the command to love is the ultimate moral principle of all human relationships. But they lacked what some Greek moralists called "middle axioms" which were:

. . . those subordinate maxims which connect the ultimate principles with the complexities of the actual historical situations in which action has to be taken.[35]

Or:

. . . maxims of conduct which mediate between the fundamental principles and the tangle of particular problems.[36]

For Temple, as for Oldham, the middle axioms were important as being of intermediate specificity.

Temple seemed to think that the formulation of middle axioms was a task of an assembled company of Christians. He told the company gathered at Malvern that while they would not be able to supply the great need for these principles, they would be able to record what agreement there was.[37] Bennett's usage of the term in the early 1940's also had this connotation. The middle axioms were "less pretentious" than Roman

[33] *CR,* pp. 112–115.
[34] Bennett, "Christian Concerns," a farewell sermon preached at the First Congregational Church of Berkeley, California, on June 20, 1943, and printed in pamphlet form, pp. 5–6.
[35] Temple, in *Malvern, 1941,* p. 10. It is not clear which Greek moralists Temple had in mind.
[36] *Ibid.,* p. vii.
[37] *Ibid.,* p. 10.

Catholic natural law, he said, because they did not claim to have universal validity. The existence of relevant middle axioms at a given time "can only be determined by the success that Christians have in arriving at a consensus."[38] He admitted what other scholars have since noticed, that the term was misleading, "because it suggests a greater degree of self-evidence than is justified."[39]

Another way of seeing what is involved in the middle axiom proposal is by examining what its sponsor believes to be the major Protestant alternatives.

The first, and least satisfactory, of these is a radical separation of the Christian standards from public decisions. For some Lutherans and the early Barth the Christian ideal is so remote from possible realization "that its chief function is to convict us of sin and drive us all to seek forgiveness as individuals through faith in the gospel." This means the establishment of a double standard: one set of criteria for personal life, another for social life. "It abdicates from the task of relevant social criticism and leaves a moral vacuum into which flow whatever ideals happen to be approved by secular society."[40]

Setting up this kind of dichotomy is "the most disastrous of all strategies that can claim Christian support";[41] it is "moral heresy" which leads to "irresponsibility and moral paralysis when we need Christian moral guidance most of all."[42] Any strategy which suggests that there is one standard for the church or the kingdom of God and another for the civil social order is

[38] Bennett, "Results of an Ecumenical Study" (1943), p. 151.

[39] *Ibid.*, p. 147. The criticism is put sharply by Fletcher in *Situation Ethics.* He says that the term is "well meant but unfortunate, since an axiom is a self-validating, non-descriptive proposition and it cannot stand in the 'middle' between something logically prior to it and a subsequent derivative" (p. 32). In defense of the term one might say that the principles it describes are (a) "middle" in the sense of being intermediate between general and specific assertions and (b) "axioms" in the sense of being confessional, resting on faith, rather than being natural.

[40] *CR*, pp. 93–94.

[41] Bennett, "The Hardest Problem in Christian Ethics" (1943), pp. 123–124.

[42] *Ibid.*, pp. 129–130.

"fatal."[43] The development of "two independent moral standards for public and private life" is always to be avoided.[44]

The point is that Christianity must have an influence on the social principles we defend. It must govern or control them. If it did not do so, it would be irrelevant. Once translated into political terms, the Christian faith has normative consequences which cannot be ignored.

Second, one might admit the necessity of holding to these Christian norms while refusing to try to embody them in the culture at large. He would withdraw from the larger society and try to set up an enclave in which Christian standards would reign. Bennett's evaluation of this strategy has changed considerably. In the early 1940's he attributed it to the Quakers and gave them credit for a kind of action destined to raise the general moral level of society. In a world racked by war they would be the only ones everyone could trust.[45] By the late 1940's he could say that withdrawal "involves real irresponsibility because it leaves the dirty work of the world to others."[46]

While the less favorable of these assessments is probably more typical, Bennett's final judgment lies somewhere in between. He does not so much think that those who withdraw are irresponsible or malicious as he thinks they are shortsighted. A strategy of withdrawal involves a "legalisitc method of determining the involvement of the Christian in the sin of the world" and "a neglect of the larger problems of justice and world order." The exponent of withdrawal fails to see that he is obliged to consider the welfare of all and that his salvation is necessarily bound up with society as a whole. To someone who realizes these things and takes "full responsibility for the political order" such a strategy seems:

[43] *CESP*, pp. 51–57; cf. p. 53: "Whatever may be the difficulty in applying the ethic of Jesus to political life, to withhold Christian criticism of social policy is to open the door to the complete autonomy of a pagan or cynical political ethic."

[44] *FPCP*, p. 44.

[45] *CR*, pp. 94–95.

[46] *CCT* (1948–62), p. 122.

146

. . . to be dangerously complacent and legalistic. It promises holiness to a limited group at the cost of evasion of one's responsibilities as a member of the larger community. Such holiness is itself illusory, for there is real participation in the sins of the larger community that is overlooked. Christians who withdraw from the world are guilty of sins of omission that involve responsibility for evils not prevented.[47]

Thus a third strategy presented itself. It would take the form of equating the best choice available, a given social policy, with the will of God. The idea is that since God must have a will for every situation, "the best possible choice that we find available is His will."[48] There are several dangers associated with this view. It makes it hard to see that God can never simply be made the ally of one side in a social conflict. The status of those who make a different choice is called into question. There is a tendency in it to "blind oneself to the evil in one's choice."[49] Therefore this strategy could also be called a moral heresy which suggested pride and fanaticism.[50]

This heretical strategy is an especially tempting danger for liberal Protestants who often hold that "a national policy controlled by pacifist ideals is the one sound implementation of Christian ethics in international relations"—or that Christianity may be identified with the prosecution of war or a given program of economic reconstruction.[51] The danger of it is that it forgets that Christianity transcends every social institution and program (he does not say every ideal).

Thus the main problem with his strategy is that its exponent "fails to take seriously the . . . neutral issues. . . . It is these issues which make it difficult to have Christian solutions that include both goals and methods."[52] Many social judgments

[47] *CESP*, pp. 41–46.
[48] *CR*, pp. 91–93.
[49] *Ibid.*
[50] Bennett, "The Hardest Problem of Christian Ethics" (1943), p. 129.
[51] Bennett, *CESP*, p. 47. Pacifism will be discussed below in chapter 7.
[52] *Ibid.*, pp. 46–47.

147

depend on "technical knowledge which is not a part of the message of the Church" or upon "predictions of human behavior which are at best uncertain." These should be distinguished from the official message of the church.[53] Again, in *Christian Realism,* great stress was laid on the uncertainty of technical judgments and social predictions.[54] It is repeated regularly since: technical issues such as the difference between two health insurance plans and social predictions of such things as Russia's response to strong opposition are matters on which there is no characteristically Christian judgment.

Yet this is not to say that Christianity is irrelevant to such judgments. The church should "concentrate attention on the effects of any policy upon persons and remind all kinds of experts of the most important human facts by which their theories should be tested."[55] It is true that Christianity needs to ask for the judgments of experts, but:

The Christian may be more sensitive to human aspects of the situation than the expert, and he may be helped by his faith to ask deeper questions than the expert is likely to ask.[56]

Although the church has limitations involving the technical autonomy of certain problems,[57] this does not mean that she can say nothing about those problems. Bennett's formulation of the way it makes its contribution begins by making a denial of irrelevance ("dualism")[58] as well as of overconfidence ("identification").[59]

It must be noted that the problem of insufficient expertise is

[53] Bennett, "New Emphases in Christian Social Teaching" (1938), p. 530.

[54] *CR*, pp. 86–90; cf. "Enduring Bases" (1943), p. 20; the "Preface" to the new edition of *SS* written in 1946 (p. viii); and especially *CESP* (1946), pp. 28–31.

[55] *CR*, p. 30.

[56] *CC*, pp. 22–24.

[57] *CS*, p. 271; cf. Temple, *Christianity and Social Order,* pp. 16–17.

[58] *CESP*, p. 58.

[59] *CESP*, pp. 58–59; also *WCMPD*, pp. 12–18.

148

not the only reason Bennett gives for saying that God's will cannot be identified with a particular policy choice. There is another kind of reason rooted in the very nature of human social existence itself. As noted before, that existence is morally complex. It embodies a vast, historically inescapable, accumulation of disorders. A political leader is responsible to his constituents who may have different moral convictions than his and who will, in any case, demand that he serve their interests. He would be irresponsible if he did not see his obligation to them. Yet the interests of groups, especially their economic interests, inevitably conflict. Moreover political leaders tend to pretend that the interests they represent are idealistic and noble; they lack the imagination to see the needs of persons with whom they have no personal relationship. Since social reality is complicated in these ways it is inevitable that in the "public" or "social" sphere we will be obliged to do what is evil.[60] That which we are obliged to do will be detrimental to some human needs.

This complexity suggests another aspect of what Bennett means by the "transcendence" of the Christian ideal. I have already argued that he does not mean that the ideal is abstract, unattainable by definition. He means, in part, that the ideal is absolute: the Christian must always love; he must always need. But this raises a problem: if love demands that *all* the ingredients of welfare be produced (that there be both freedom and order, for example), this complete inclusiveness of the demand makes perfect love as impossible in fact as it would be if the ideal were theoretically unobtainable. Love, then, transcends a particular social decision in that it wills the elimination of the evils which are inevitably concomitant with that decision, however justifiable it may be. A concrete decision will have bad consequences; love does not will those. The Christian must move toward specificity, but his particular choice will involve a compromise of love because it will not only serve welfare, it will also create need somewhere. Thus

[60] *CESP,* pp. 17–28; see above, chapter 3.

149

Christian ethics "transcends" social policy in two ways: first, by being absolute as opposed to the shifting needs of social life; second, by being more comprehensive in its concern than a particular social and communal choice can possibly be.

Yet there are degrees of neediness. The transcendence of Christianity does not involve the Christian in being blind to certain obvious necessities of welfare. The fact is that by driving us to be concerned with need and welfare Christian ethics "*guides us in determining the goals which represent the purposes of God for our time.*" The goals are not "absolute" or "all-inclusive," but "the next steps that our own generation must take."[61] These goals are "middle axioms"; they are more concrete than a universal ethical principle and less specific than a program that includes legislation and political strategy.[62] For instance, in the case of international relations:

Notice the progression—guiding principles about which there could be no disagreement; a middle axiom which had behind it a substantial consensus but which related Christian decision to a concrete reality . . . about which there could be considerable debate . . .; and finally support of a particular program which was even more ambiguous and about which there was less agreement. Christians must move from one to three or to some equivalent of three, but as they do so the degree of authority that can be claimed in the name of Christian ethics becomes weaker with each step.[63]

Once the Christian perspective has been translated into political terms its consequences still have to be spelled out. The Christian may claim the support of his faith for the first stages of his process, for certain things that are generally needed now. He is on much shakier ground when it comes to making a specific decision.

At precisely this point Bennett's book was greeted with a vigorous critique. Writing in *Christendom,* Peter Bertocci

[61] *CESP,* pp. 76–77.
[62] *CESP,* pp. 77–85.
[63] *CESP,* p. 79.

argued that Bennett's claim that the Christian ideal transcended every social policy or program "may take the moral nerve out of Christian action." This was because, on Bennett's terms, "Christian ethics is unimpeachable in transcendent principle, but . . . the closer the Christian gets to the situation which confronts the individual the less he can be sure that he is being a good Christian!" Bennett's theory saves "the purity of the principle, but not the confidence in our ability, or God's ability through us, to enact it in the best possible manner in that situation."[64]

Bertocci himself questioned whether a Christian social ethic should be "the statement of principles whose specific connections with any particular situation must always be doubtfully relevant." The notion of a transcendent ideal made more and more relevant should be discarded in favor of procedural criteria. Christians should stand for "the *ideal of democratic method*" which does not balk at equating God's will with what men freely decide to do.[65]

For Bennett this option represented an unjustifiable equation of a particular decision with God's will. Unless the Christian contribution is clearest at the more general levels it is impossible to include the manifold divergence at the level of particular choice within the Christian umbrella. Thus:

. . . suppose that Professor Bertocci tried to show just what guidance there is in Christian ethics for those who do as a matter of fact come to different judgments on technical and other neutral issues, he would be forced to distinguish, as I have tried to do, between the Christian elements that go into the making of decisions and those more precarious elements about which there is no Christian certainty. In my book it was my intention to put together the kind of guidance that Churches can give to their members.[66]

[64] Peter Bertocci, "A Sixth Conception of Christian Strategy: A Critique of John C. Bennett's *Christian Ethics and Social Policy*" in *Christendom*, XIII (1948), pp. 48–49.

[65] *Ibid.*, p. 50.

[66] Bennett, "Comment" in *Christendom*, XIII (1948), p. 56.

Thus, as Paul Lehmann said, Bennett was concerned with "the highly significant question of the relation between the social imperative and the social strategy of the Christian ethic."[67] When he considers alternative strategies and makes the middle axiom proposal he has not, from the very first, meant to be solving the question of natural law. He does treat that question, as we have seen, but at a different point. The question of middle axioms is not a question of epistemology but of specificity. Thus, as a historical point of some interest, the main concern of *Christian Ethics and Social Policy* is quite different from that of H. Richard Niebuhr's later work *Christ and Culture*. There are various overlaps, it is true, but the problematic is quite different.

Niebuhr was concerned, among other things, with the relationship between the revealed and the natural, between love and justice. Of course this does not exhaust the concerns of his book since "culture" is defined very broadly indeed.[68] But his overriding concern was with the relationship between two authorities;[69] Bennett's problem is the proper behavior for one institution. Bennett's question is, "How specifically may I formulate the consequences of my faith?"; Niebuhr's is, "What is the relationship between my faith and non-faith?"

The concern represented by the "middle axiom" phrase has continued, but Bennett's dissatisfaction with the term, already noted, manifests itself in unwillingness to use it at every opportunity. He deals with the problem without use of the phrase in an essay on economics[70] and it never appears in his most comprehensive recent book, *Christians and the State,* which is, essentially, a lengthy elaboration of some middle axioms of social and political life.

Yet he has not given up the concept. He returned to it in

[67] Paul Lehmann, Review of *CESP* (1948), pp. 447–448. Lehmann, incidentally, was very appreciative of the middle axiom idea, which he thought "significantly extended the frontier of Christian social thinking."
[68] H. Richard Niebuhr, *Christ and Culture* (New York, 1951), p. 31.
[69] *Ibid.*, p. 11.
[70] Bennett, Christian Ethics and Economic Life" (1954), pp. 302–303.

The Christian as Citizen in 1955. He repeats the quotation from Oldham and says that it means that middle axioms are "more definite than a universal ethical principle" and "less specific" than legislative programs.[71] They are "definite goals," "immediate objectives" or "proximate goals." The process of defining them consists primarily of the elimination of viable alternatives. They are to be understood to be tentative, not absolute: "no formulation of these objectives should be allowed to harden, or . . . be regarded as a kind of Christian law."[72]

Writing for an international audience (the book was published for the International Missionary Council), Bennett stressed the fact that diverse geographical situations might require the formation of different middle axioms for different places. Some of the axioms "may be relevant to a particular region rather than to the whole world."[73] The reason for this was the unlikelihood "that those whose responsibility and experiences profoundly differ will reach identical views on policy." This did not make the attempt to formulate middle axioms useless, because the recognition that such principles could be formulated at all showed some measure of agreement, of consensus. It established the existence of generally acknowledged standards in the light of which a healthy kind of disagreement was possible. Such a healthy ethos was possible on the basis of "the frankest recognition of the way in which the differences of conviction are brought about by differences of experience."[74]

Bennett's most recent defense of the middle axiom proposal is in an essay circulated in various forms,[75] but which I know as the presidential address to the American Society of Christian

[71] *CC*, p. 39.
[72] *CC*, p. 43.
[73] *CC*, pp. 39–40.
[74] *CC*, p. 44.
[75] Paul Lehmann in *Ethics in a Christian Context* (New York, 1963), pp. 148–154, knows the essay in an earlier form. The writer must confess that he finds Professor Lehmann's criticism of Bennett's proposal to be very obscure.

153

Social Ethics of 1961. It is called "Principles and the Context."
This essay contains a distinction between normative and descriptive middle axioms. Both are kinds of "more specific objectives which belong to particular historical periods," but such principles may be either (a) objectives proper, or (b) "descriptions of some condition of which policy must take account." As an example of (b) a descriptive middle axiom, Bennett suggests the judgment that segregation is a form of discrimination. In relation to this the normative middle axiom, (a), would be the command to overcome involuntary racial segregation. In this context the broad judgment presupposed is the wrongness of racial discrimination. While Bennett has not stressed this distinction, it does show that both judgments of fact and moral principles are ingredients in the formulation of middle axioms.[76]

Bennett repeats his insistence that middle axioms are important because of the particular referent they involve. They are claims that the church can safely make now. His reason for distinguishing them from policy is revealing:

. . . there can often be agreement on these "middle axioms" when there is no agreement on policy and such agreement may greatly help to form a common mind in Church and community which will prepare the way for agreement on policy later.

Agreement on middle axioms allows the church "more effectively to encourage its members and many voluntary groups to experiment with the support of specific policies."[77]

For Bennett the middle axioms are, although "not exclusively Christian," an instrument of the church. They are "implied in Christian faith and ethics."[78] They are the very stuff of the church's social education. Less important than their basis in

[76] Bennett, "Principles and the Context" (1961), pp. 12–13. In a letter to the writer Bennett says that James Luther Adams taught him this distinction.
[77] *Ibid.*, p. 13.
[78] *Ibid.*, pp. 13–14.

the perspective and broad social principles, they give those generalities essential specificity. Without them the church's message would be general and easily ignored. With them she becomes the aid of the oppressed and the needy, the guardian of the public welfare.

In summary, Bennett's understanding of the transition from Christian faith to political decision can be schematized as follows. It involves a translation by the church from the language of faith to the language of politics and then, secondly, a specification of what in concrete circumstances is required. The *translation* is accomplished because the Christian faith and ethic require that welfare be secured—yet needs must be articulated in political terms. The specification involves judgments about what is necessary here and now, there and then. In order to see, for example, what combination of order and freedom a given society requires one must see what will serve its welfare.

Judgments about welfare, in other words, link not only the language of faith and the language of politics; they also link generally important political criteria to concrete situations. Given that welfare, in principle, involves order, freedom, and justice, the church must perceive the realities of a given situation and then formulate norms for it in terms of these broad criteria. Those norms, relevant to only as large an area as one can safely generalize about, are called middle axioms.

Consequently, the last stage in a Christian social ethic consists of the formulation by the church of these middle axioms on the basis of (a) the perspective and broad criteria and (b) judgments of factual need. The final expository section of this book will examine some of the principles Bennett has defended on this level. It must be stressed that no claim for comprehensiveness is made at this stage. By no means is Bennett consistent in the middle axioms he lists—a fact which is obviously consistent with his theory. In 1943 he listed as

155

definitely Christian social objectives the establishment of world government, abolition of racial discrimination, and the securing of full employment and political freedom.[79] In the same year he specifically listed as "middle axioms" these same points with the addition of the provision of welfare allowances and the reform of the property system short of abolition of the right of private property.[80] In *The Christian as Citizen* he lists land reform in underdeveloped countries, the ending of racial segregation, the prevention of unemployment, and self-government for peoples now under foreign rule.[81] In "Principles and the Context" the list includes desegregation, the prevention of nuclear war, restriction of the arms race, support of the open and pluralistic society, and insistence that government should be responsible for a stable economy.[82]

These lists may suggest the scope of the issues that have engaged Professor Bennett over a long career of church leadership. This author will make no effort to recite the whole of his social comment. Instead it seems of more interest to concentrate attention on one topic with which he has constantly been concerned: foreign policy.

[79] Bennett, "Enduring Bases" (1943), p. 27.
[80] Bennett, "Christian Concerns" (1943), *passim.*
[81] *CC*, pp. 40–43.
[82] Bennett, "Principles and the Context" (1961), p. 13.

7. THE CHRISTIAN PERSPECTIVE ON FOREIGN POLICY

Christianity can not dissociate itself from the needs of those in other countries. There is no escape in the Christian faith from wrestling with the dilemmas of foreign policy. This means that Christians have to reason about these problems, like everyone else, but it further means that foreign policy calculations must be kept "under a continuous Christian judgement."[1]

During the Second World War the churches evolved a rather consistent and "non-pacifist" way of accomplishing this. Their attitude was "controlled by the recognition that the War was itself the result of an historical situation to which all the great powers had contributed." Therefore those who appeared as enemies could be understood to be caught in one side of a tragic historical situation. Christians in this country felt bonds of loyalty with Christians in the enemy lands—a feeling to which the World Council of Churches (in process of formation) contributed greatly. Within the churches themselves there was considerable concern with certain moral issues raised by the conduct of the war. There was "a general desire to keep the symbols of the faith and the church's worship as free as possible from the military symbols and from the spirit generated by the war" as well as "a far more ungrudging acceptance of the role of conscientious objectors" than in World War I. Finally churchmen realized that the war had, at best, a negative func-

[1] *CS*, p. 173.

157

tion of halting aggression, that "it could not of itself produce a positive result."[2]

The fundamental consideration was that the national interest could never be ultimate for the Christian or for the church. National loyalty was important, but stress on it "can never justify the tendency to make national interest the ultimate point of reference or to assume that God cares more about the interests of one's own nation than for those of other nations." In other words "Christians should be more concerned about the solidarity of men in Christ than they are about their relationship to a nation . . ."[3] While Bennett has consistently held that national interest is an important guideline in international politics he has, since it is not ultimate, regularly argued that those aspects of the national interest which other nations have in common with us should be stressed. The existent mutualities of interest should be emphasized. The national interest must be understood in a broad, imaginative, long-range way. Since in the long run men have a common fate, differences of national interest will be minimized in this context. Christians should argue for a foreign policy controlled by national interest in this sense; their first loyalty is to the interests of humanity as a whole rather than to the nation.[4]

In this context it seems almost ludicrous that Bennett has been criticized for holding that the nation is "both point of departure and destination" for ethical reasoning about foreign policy. For Bennett, as for his challenger, the church is "the framework of actual political meaning and commitment." Because the church exists, because men have loyalties that tran-

---

[2] CS, pp. 175–178. For Bennett's fidelity to these standards during the war see Bennett, "In Such A Time" in Christendom, VIII (1942), pp. 162–168 and Bennett, "A Christian Perspective on the War" in The Friend, CXII, No. 3 (March, 1942), pp. 29–31.

[3] CS, p. 183; cf. Bennett, "Enduring Bases" (1943), p. 32.

[4] Bennett discusses the relativity of national interest at many places. See among others: CESP, pp. 63–65; CS, pp. 181–186; FPCP, pp. 54–64.

scend that to the nation, they can suggest specific modifications in the nation's understanding of its true interest.[5]

What the church is to do in order to affect the behavior of the nation is a further problem. As we have seen, the church has an indirect role because it is a universal community relating people separated by national boundaries. Thus through its corridors much information is exchanged. Because it exists as an international fellowship the church in fact affects the way the nation appraises its interests.[6]

Second, and more important, the church as a body within the nation must bring its perspective to bear upon questions of national foreign policy. Of course the deepest service the church can render to the nation is to be itself and mediate the Gospel, but the Gospel "needs to be interpreted in ways that are relevant to the international situation."[7] The churches must teach about international affairs. The basis for that teaching is the whole Christian perspective which suggests the importance of the other's welfare and the limited character of international achievements.

But what right has the church to speak about the technicalities of foreign policy? The church has this right because those who make decisions about foreign policy are not governed "except in very limited areas of tactics and timing" by their possession of privileged data. Rather their judgments are formed by their "broad pictures of the world" including, for instance, their judgments about the dynamics of Communism.[8]

[5] Cf. Paul Peachey, Book Review of John C. Bennett, ed., *Nuclear Weapons and the Conflict of Conscience in The Christian Century,* May 23, 1962, p. 661; for Bennett's views on world government see among other locations: CS, pp. 190–192; CESP, pp. 77–79; WCMPD, pp. 74–75; FPCP, pp. 127–143.

[6] *FPCP,* pp. 144–149; see above, chapter 5.

[7] *FPCP,* p. 152.

[8] In fact Bennett thinks: ". . . it is probably true that at the present time the tougher elements in foreign policy are so well established and have so much support from what President Eisenhower in an inspired moment called the 'military industrial complex' that the churches have

In other words, the decisive questions about foreign policy are not questions that are settled on the basis of expertise. Rather they are questions settled on the basis of perspectives which must be defended in the sphere of public debate in which the church takes a part; the "ethical sensitivities that come from the experience of the universal Church should have an affect on this debate" by keeping men aware of the needs of others.[9]

Since Christian criticism is legitimate, what forms should it take? In a recent article Bennett lists "six areas in which persons who combine religious perspectives and moral sensitivity with a careful attempt to understand the relevant facts, though not specialists or insiders in the government, have a right and duty to speak."[10] Such citizens have "a right and a duty to call attention to the immediate human consequences of any policy." Further they may question the goals of a given policy and the means used to attain those goals. They must help their fellow citizens see the world as it appears to those in other lands (a responsibility which, while it does not suggest that they "have a monopoly of wisdom concerning the more intangible effects of our policies," rests on the notion that "they do have an inside track to this kind of understanding. . . .") The churches may question the presuppositions of a given policy and they must "criticize the false uses of religion and morality that are so common."[11]

Obviously in Bennett's terms a significant range of foreign policy questions falls within the competence of the church. What has he understood that the church should say about these questions? As we have said, he now defends a policy of "non-pacifism," but it was not always so.

----

been right in putting the emphasis on the elements which the government is most tempted to neglect" (*FPCP*, pp. 158–159).

[9] *FPCP*, pp. 21–24.

[10] Bennett, "The Issue of Peace: The Voice of Religion" in *Worldview*, IX, No. 4 (April, 1966), p. 5. This same essay appears in *Representative American Speeches 1965–66*, ed. Lester Thonssen (New York, 1966), pp. 142–155. I quote from the *Worldview* article.

[11] *Ibid.*, pp. 5–7; cf. Bennett, "Christian Realism in Vietnam" in *America*, CXIV, No. 18 (April 30, 1966), p. 66.

In the 1930's Bennett was a pacifist. In 1930 he wrote an article for *The Christian Century* called "Can Armistice Sunday be Saved?" He denounced military pomp within the church's service of worship:

The very celebration which took place yesterday, the speeches of the orators show that among us there is the same unteachable patriotism, the same love of military display, the same trust in military preparedness so often proved wrong, the same willingness to subordinate the Church to the nation.[12]

The bellicose emotions now connected with Armistice Sunday must, he said, be transmuted into a "positive determination to end all war." The churches should encourage us to think of those who had died in war not as heroes but as victims. There should be no distinction drawn between German and Allied dead.[13]

Bennett insisted on pacifism in domestic as well as international action. His differences with Reinhold Niebuhr on this point came out as early as 1933 when the Fellowship of Reconciliation sent out a questionnaire to its members. The questions concerned use of violence as a means to social reform. The result was a rupture in the Fellowship.

The questionnaire was worded like this: in seeking social reform members should "go as far as to":

1. Proclaim the ideal . . . through methods of love, moral suasion and education, but refuse to identify themselves with either . . . class. . . .
2. Identify themselves . . . and protest against the use of violence by the police, militia and underprivileged . . . distribute relief to workers striking . . .; attempt peacefully to maintain civil liberties . . . but without the use of any form of coercion.
3. Assist in organizing workers into unions and in leading them in

[12] Bennett, "Can Armistice Sunday be Saved?" in *The Christian Century*, XLVII, Part 2 (November 26, 1930), p. 1444.
[13] *Ibid.*, pp. 1444–1445.

161

strikes . . . and if need be in a non-violent general strike; assist in organizing the workers into a political party which will use non-violent measures . . . dissociating themselves from any group that used armed violence.

4. In case the legal owners of essential industries resort to armed force if necessary to secure the advantage of the workers, but the workers . . . in . . . non-violent ways.

5. In the situation described in #4 consent to the use of armed force . . . refuse to use violence against them but offer to serve regretfully and only while the necessity for it continues.

6. In anticipation of general class warfare, assist in the arming of workers . . .; when war is fully joined, urge workers to acts of violence and participate with them. . . .[14]

Many more members of the FOR chose #4 than any of the other positions; #5 and #6 were distinctly unpopular. Since this was the case Niebuhr felt that he must resign. He had to go beyond the prohibition of violence because he regarded "all problems of social morality in pragmatic rather than absolute terms." Moral prohibitions on the use of violence by the workers would "give an undue advantage to that portion of the community which is always using non-violent coercion against the disinherited.[15] The Christian law of love could not be an absolute guide in social morality. It was something always to be striven for; thus it required the repudiation of hatred but not of violence:

Recognizing, as liberal Christianity does not, that the world of politics is full of demonic forces we have chosen on the whole to support the devil of vengeance against the devil of hypocrisy. In the days in which we live a dying social system commits the hypocrisy of hiding its injustices behind the forms of justice and its victims

[14] Quoted in Donald Meyer, *The Protestant Search for Political Realism 1919–1941* (Berkeley, 1960), p. 205.
[15] Reinhold Niebuhr, "Why I Leave the FOR" in *The Christian Century*, LI (January 3, 1934), p. 18.

162

of injustice express their politics in terms of resentment against this injustice.[16]

Niebuhr's reaction did not go without a response. Charles Clayton Morrison said that it was certainly not based on pragmatism but on a dogmatic kind of Communism.[17]

Yet it received an even more forceful, if proleptic, rejoinder. Writing in *The World Tomorrow* John Bennett claimed that the issues raised by the questionnaire were not those of principle at all. It raised issues with regard to which "our surest principles seem to be capable of being heard on both sides of the question, depending upon our interpretation of the facts." Pacifists might, for instance, argue that "revolutionary action might be too destructive" and in doing so they would not be raising questions of principle so much as those of "the consequences of a revolutionary strategy."[18]

The particular positions on the questionnaire had varying merits. It would be intolerable to go along with position #1 and remain neutral in the class struggle since in comparison with the claims of the privileged the aspirations of the workers are "much closer to an objective justice."[19]

Positions #5 and #6 were hard to differentiate and of the two the sixth was preferable since:

If we are to go on the assumption that in the crisis we are to use armed force, the sooner that we prepare for it the better, both in providing arms and in disciplining people for the war.

But this whole approach was *unrealistic*. The advocacy of violence on the part of the workers would serve to hinder, not to help, their cause. Class-conscious workers would always be

---

[16] *Ibid.*, p. 19.
[17] Charles Clayton Morrison in *The Christian Century*, LI (January 10, 1934), pp. 47–48.
[18] Bennett, "That Fellowship Questionnaire" in *The World Tomorrow*, XVI (December 21, 1933), p. 690.
[19] *Ibid.*, p. 691.

in the minority in America and for them to threaten to use violence would only consolidate the opposition to them. Against them stands the great military power of the state. Further, in a true class war the forces of destruction would get out of control; there would be nothing of value left for the workers to capture. The order that could be built on the basis of violent conquest could only be sustained by violent imposition. Finally, the possibilities of non-violence and persuasion had by no means been exhausted.[20]

Once the last two positions had been eliminated on the grounds that they would not succeed, Bennett was left with positions #2, #3, and #4. These, he thought, represented legitimate differences of emphasis in one sound strategy which was neither detached nor self-defeating. He admitted that one consequence would be unplanned violence. Accepting its inevitability, however, did not lessen its undesirability or decrease the importance of persuasion:

No matter what position we take about coercion, we all believe, when we think in terms of total strategy, that unless the majority of the middle-class people are persuaded to consent to social change, the new order can only be given stability by a ruthlessness which will poison it. . . . Peaceful revolution will only be possible if whenever we assert the necessity of coercion we also assert that we cannot set definite limits to the power of moral forces in history.[21]

Thus Bennett insisted on non-violence in the class-struggle. But his major point of attack was still international conflict. In

[20] *Ibid.* On the basis of Bennett's analysis this writer finds it hard to see how Donald Meyer (in *The Protestant Search for Political Realism 1919–1941*, p. 209) can conclude that the difference between positions #4 and #5 on the questionnaire *necessarily* represented a difference *in principle*. Bennett's rejection of positions #5 and #6 was pragmatic, and, so it seems to me, based on a more sensitive analysis of the possible consequences than Niebuhr's "pragmatic" answer. Here as elsewhere in this invaluable book Meyer's judgments are distorted by his desire to isolate Niebuhr as *the* truly realistic political philosopher against a background made up of many much lesser lights.

[21] Bennett, "That Fellowship Questionnaire" (1933), pp. 691–692.

1934 in a letter to *The World Tomorrow* he argued for the need for a new anti-war organization which would have a broader base than the existent radical organizations. There was much nascent support for such a movement he claimed and preoccupation with certain specific issues was no longer sufficient to rally it. The movement should stand for non-participation in international war and "realism" about the relationship which existed between capitalism and war. Yet it should be separate from such radical movements as socialism and Communism and should strive to co-operate with other agencies which are striving to build peace machinery. In other words, the movement must be broad enough to include people who are disillusioned with capitalism but who are unready to support socialism because "we haven't time to convert them to socialism before we organize them against war."[22]

Although his dissatisfaction with pacifism was beginning to show through,[23] in *Christianity—And Our World* (1936), Bennett still argued that war was not only a "futile horror" but was "peculiarly in contradiction to all that Christianity means because of what it makes persons do to persons." Christians, therefore:

. . . can no longer follow blindly their governments into all wars. This is an application of the general principle that Christians owe their first allegiance to God and to the welfare of the whole human community and not to the state.[24]

Bennett went on to distinguish among kinds of pacifism. He clearly preferred the position of "pragmatic pacifists" who "base their opposition to war on their belief that no conceivable war would have consequences which would be worth the cost" to

---

[22] Bennett, Letter to the editor of *The World Tomorrow* published under the title, "Calling for a New United Front" in *The World Tomorrow*, XVII (January 4, 1934), pp. 21–22.

[23] *CAOW*, pp. 58–59.

[24] *CAOW*, pp. 56–57.

that of "absolute pacifists" who "reject all organized violence against persons as inherently and inevitably wrong."[25]

In 1937 and 1938 Bennett was still defending pacifism, evidently on pragmatic grounds. War was repudiated because of its heinous effects in 1937.[26] By 1938 he could admit that there might be worse things than the physical destruction associated with war, "but it would be difficult to point to anything worse than war which is not, in large part, a result of war." Specifically, it was "an illusion to suppose that by war Fascism can be destroyed or its victims saved."[27]

But this argument for pacifism would break down if it could be shown that refusal to go to war would cause greater harm than war itself. During the next four years John Bennett came to realize that the world confronted the danger of something worse than war. This change of mind about what the greater evil was, was recorded in a series of four exchanges with *The Christian Century*.

In 1939 Bennett defended American neutrality in the coming Second World War. He could not go along with those who suggested that the decision for neutrality was an obvious or easy one. Instead the decision was tragic because we could not have suggested to the English a way to stay out of the war.[28] Once that was said, it had to be added that the war could be

[25] *CAOW*, p. 58. In the preface to the second edition of *SS* (1946) Bennett says of himself: "I was not an absolute pacifist in 1935, but then I could not imagine a greater evil than war" (*SS*, p. viii). In later writings Bennett distinguishes between pacifists who claim that pacifism is a political alternative and those who do not make that claim. He directs his argument only against the former; the latter are handled under the rubric of "Strategies of Withdrawal" in *CESP*. (Cf. *CS*, pp. 167–169; *FPCP*, pp. 26–27.) I assume that this later distinction is different from the earlier one; the absolute-pragmatic distinction refers to the grounds on which pacifism is justified while the policy-no policy distinction refers to the range within which pacifism should be applicable.

[26] Bennett, "Religious Foundation" (1937), p. 8.

[27] Bennett, "Christians and the International Crisis" in *Christendom*, IV (1939), pp. 178–180.

[28] Bennett, "Neutrality: The Christian's Dilemma" in *The Christian Century*, LVI (November 1, 1939), p. 1329.

viewed in three contexts. If one considered only the events since Munich or the occupation of Prague, then Hitler bore the guilt for the war and the case for our intervention would be strong. But one must also consider the hostilities in the context of events since 1918 and, in this context, "Hitlerism is but a symptom of a national neurosis that has definite causes for which the Allies themselves are largely responsible." Finally, one must see the war in the context of the results that can be expected to issue from it. The only way that Hitlerism would be overcome would be by an invasion from the West and such an invasion would seem to the Germans to be an aggressive war. Such a war would *"strengthen* the tendencies which have given Hitler power."[29]

The final context was decisive. "This war cannot be expected to accomplish the war aims of the Allies." Furthermore, although it is "not a great good," it is "good to keep this hemisphere out of war." Moreover, by remaining neutral we preserve sanity and the ability to find conditions which could lead to a negotiated peace.[30]

Controversy began when the *Century* used this article for its own polemical purposes. In an editorial it responded to a group of Christians (five pacifists and five non-pacifists) in New York City—Bennett was in California at this time—who, while acknowledging their differences, said that in judgments about the growing European conflict "virtually all thoughtful Christians" were agreed. The *Century* quoted Bennett's article to show that this was not so; not all thoughtful Christians were in agreement.[31]

Bennett responded in a letter which the *Century* printed under the title "From One Illusion to Another." He said he had changed his mind about the consequences of a German victory. When he wrote his earlier article he was "living under an illusion." He had assumed that "the most we had to fear

[29] *Ibid.*, pp. 1329–1331.
[30] *Ibid.*, p. 1331.
[31] *The Christian Century*, LVII (September 4, 1940), pp. 1070–1071.

was an exhausting stalemate or a victory for the Allies." He had not realized that "a German victory would mean something new to modern man—the extension of political tyranny by means of military conquest."[32]

To guard against that evil Bennett advocated what he called "selective intervention." Britain should be defended "in the interest of justice, freedom, and our security" in ways that did not compromise "our freedom of action in case Britain later seeks to invade the continent." Saving Britain was one thing; "the quixotic task of trying to save the continent of Europe from itself by military force" was another. Such an attempt would be futile as all wars are futile. Our "chief contribution to democracy should be the improvement of our own institutions and way of life" rather than "participation in European civil wars and . . . the policing of Europe."[33]

The *Century* did not take this lying down. "We prefer to appeal from John Bennett, a momentary victim of war hysteria, to John Bennett, the objective analyst of war realities." The concept of "selective intervention" was only a "euphemism" for war. If the cause was just, there should be no limit to our involvement. Bennett had "cast off one illusion only to embrace another" and had "fallen into an unintelligible jumble of self-contradictory ideas."[34]

Evidently this tirade did not force Bennett to give up the idea of partial involvement. Later in the same year he wrote again for the *Century*. Noting that his advocacy of neutrality had always been because it was the lesser of two evils, he admitted that the increasing threat of German victory had forced him to realize that "the world today is threatened by something far more dangerous than a German victory [in World

[32] Bennett, Letter to the editor of *The Christian Century* published with the title: "From One Illusion to Another" in *The Christian Century*, LVII (September 18, 1940), p. 1146.

[33] *Ibid.*, p. 1147.

[34] *The Christian Century*, LVII (September 18, 1940), p. 1147.

War I] . . . and far more disastrous than the peace of Versailles."[35] Naziism was evil. It was reactionary in discarding the vast gains of the past. Of course it could not last indefinitely, but that did not mean that it could not last long enough to do tremendous harm. However much it might be true that this tyranny was a manifestation of God's judgment, such rationalizations should not be made into justifications for the complacency of observers.[36]

Pacifism as a policy for our nation had to be decisively rejected, since it would encourage German victory. The alternative was not full participation. The United States should "give the most important aid to Britain and China now without declaring war and without assuming . . . unlimited liability. . . ." American destiny should not be identified with what happened in Europe. But, if these policies led this country to war, then the war must be supported.[37]

Bennett affirmed this conclusion even more strongly in 1941. He had, he said, "no hesitation in saying that it is God's will that we do all that we can to defeat the Nazi power."[38] While the war is not holy, it is just; it is not beyond criticism. Our own nation is guilty, but what should be emphasized now is "the overwhelming importance of overcoming the threat of the Nazis to the world." The war might not be exactly good, but it was right; it involved evil but it was the most justifiable action. To say this might seem like "throwing dust, but the human situation is not simple and what is its inescapable complexity may appear to be dust to some observers."[39]

After Pearl Harbor Bennett was even more certain. There

[35] Bennett, "If America Enters the War" in *The Christian Century*, LVII (December 4, 1940), p. 1506.

[36] *Ibid.*, pp. 1506–1507.

[37] *Ibid.*, pp. 1507–1508.

[38] Bennett, Letter to the editor of *The Christian Century*, published as "Not a Holy War" in *The Christian Century*, LVIII (October 8, 1941), pp. 1243–1244.

[39] *Ibid.*; cf. The Christian Century, "Is War Holy?" in *The Christian Century*, LVIII (October 8, 1940), pp. 1230–1231.

was no use in speculating about what the shape of the post-war world should be, he said, until we realized that the new order, to have hope, must rest on a decisive defeat for the Axis.[40] Of course our motives for involvement were mixed, but the "objective situation" was that "our victory would mean the end of slavery for many nations." Our cause was just in the sense that "we are the only instruments available for overcoming a form of power that is monstrously unjust and which lacks the means of self-criticism and self-correction which keep our forms of injustice from being enemies of hope."[41] The church should make clear that Christians have a stake in the war; American soldiers should not simply be told that they are "victims of a common tragedy or of God's judgment." They could be told that their deaths would "insure justice and freedom." Their situation was significantly different from that of the men drafted by the Germans and other Axis powers and they should not be deprived of this legitimate source of morale.[42]

Thus, in fact, John Bennett gave up his pacifism. But what arguments has he used on a more abstract level?

Consistent pacifism had to make three affirmations. First, that violence which had as its objective the taking of human life was always to be renounced. Second, that such violence was always self-defeating. Third, that there is a positive and non-violent strategy for implementing the Christian ethic in most, if not all, situations.[43] Pacifism which says these things has much to recommend it. The disillusionment about war which underlies the pacifist movement is, on the whole, to the good. It is not sufficient to challenge the pacifist with the pervasiveness of sin because that doctrine also limits what one can

[40] Bennett, "Revolution or Counter-Revolution" (1942), p. 209.
[41] Bennett, Editorial: "A False Christian Nationalism" in *Christianity and Crisis*, II, No. 4 (March 23, 1942), p. 6.
[42] Bennett, Editorial: "The Churches and the War" in *Christianity and Crisis*, II, No. 15 (September 21, 1942), pp. 1–2; compare with the reference at n. 19 above.
[43] *CR*, pp. 99–100.

expect from engaging in violence.[44] To this day Bennett can agree that the burden of proof is on the non-pacifist.[45]

Yet for at least twenty-five years Bennett has held that it is a burden that can be borne. At one time he argued that pacifism was associated with isolationism—a charge he no longer makes.[46] But there are other serious flaws with the pacifist position as a political strategy.

In the first place, pacifism rests on an oversimplification of the commandment to love:

> Christian love involves a double imperative. On the one hand it is an imperative against violence; but, also, it makes us responsible for the restraint of evil.[47]

In concrete situations these imperatives may conflict. In a situation in which violence is already in progress this may mean that one must use further violence in order to get the best result; if violence is threatened, one may have to threaten to use violence to prevent it. Consequently:

> Those who are under the imperative of love must often face the fact that if they heed only the warning against violence, they may in some cases become responsible for the evil that might have been restrained had they acted in time.[48]

This remains Bennett's fundamental objection to pacifism, even in the face of the threat of nuclear war. There are other evils

---

[44] Bennett, "The Christian Faith and Political Strategy" in *Christianity and Crisis*, I, No. 2 (February 24, 1941), p. 3.

[45] *WCMPD*, p. 76.

[46] Bennett, "Faith and Strategy" (1941), p. 3; cf. the response by Oscar J. F. Seitz in *Christianity and Crisis*, I, No. 6 (April 21, 1941), p. 8. Bennett dropped the assertion of a link between pacifism and isolationism in *CR*. But he retained the affirmation that: "I do not believe that pacifists, especially in America, face the problem that arises when they themselves do not bear the brunt of the suffering to which their policy of non-violence may contribute" (*CR*, p. 108).

[47] *CR*, p. 101.

[48] *CR*, p. 104.

which one should try to prevent besides the evil of war.[49] The pacifist makes the mistake of translating love into the language of only one social value.

Second, pacifism is unrealistic. No nation can be expected to have the moral discipline to refuse to defend itself.[50] This is true today in the United States,[51] even in the face of the threat of nuclear destruction. A government is the trustee for the security of its people and the American people interpret their security in a way that requires military defense.[52]

Third, it is not always possible to act in a way which will avoid responsibility for the taking of human life. A strategy of non-violence is not always available.[53] For instance, confronted with the European war, one could not decide that no one was going to be killed. He had the choice of doing what he could so that the result of the killing was an improved situation or of allowing events to take their course without his action. But the course events were taking involved a great deal of killing. Pacifism had no guidance to offer in such a situation. Therefore, for all these reasons, it was not a "self-sufficient social strategy available at all times to the nation and to those who are responsible for public policy."[54]

Pacifism, in Bennett's terms, does not so much make a theoretical mistake as a factual one. The pacifist tends to think that all men need is peace, that everyone is agreed that this is true, and that peace is always a possibility. Since none of these judgments is necessarily or always correct, pacifism is not necessarily or always the best Christian social policy. But it might sometimes be the right strategy. Bennett has never wanted to suggest that there might not be times in which pacifism, the renunciation of violence, is the policy most productive of welfare. But to advocate a pacifist policy at any

[49] Cf. *CS*, pp. 169–171; *WCMPD*, p. 77; *FPCP*, pp. 29–30, 110–111.
[50] *CR*, pp. 104–106.
[51] *FPCP*, pp. 27–29.
[52] *FPCP*, p. 111.
[53] *CR*, pp. 106–108.
[54] *CR*, p. 101; the original is in italics.

given time one must be able to show that "a pacifist policy is the best method of getting the best results in the long run, all things considered."[55]

Conversely the non-pacifist must always be able to show that more good than harm will come from the policy he advocates. Pacifism is never excluded *in principle* as a policy alternative. Just how seriously Bennett takes this comes out in his discussion of nuclear pacifism. The evil consequences of the arms race (to be discussed below) create a situation in which it is not obvious that the possession by the United States of deterrent power is worthwhile.[56] Radical disarmament is a "reasonable goal, however difficult it may be to achieve and to maintain it."[57] These things seem to suggest that in the present state of military technology war is always the greatest evil.[58]

"The case for this is strong but not conclusive."[59] Although it is uncertain that unilateral nuclear disarmament would invite aggression, the chances are that our government will not adopt such a policy and if it did the result might be delayed multilateral disarmament.[60] The pacifism of the 1960's is more helpful than that of the late 1930's, but it tends to play down too much the role of the deterrent capacity of the United States.[61] Therefore, since our government will not in fact adopt such a policy and since, because of the possible consequences, one cannot be certain that it ought to, nuclear pacifism is not a "self-sufficient policy." Someone who advocates it must "recognize the need of an interim strategy that takes account of the responsibilities of government in the situation as it is." The nuclear pacifist is free to try to make his policy applicable by bringing about a revolution in public opinion, but Bennett is

[55] *CESP*, p. 47.
[56] Bennett, "How My Mind Has Changed" (1959), p. 1502.
[57] Bennett, "Moral Tensions" (1964), p. 26.
[58] *FPCP*, p. 50.
[59] *Ibid.*
[60] Bennett, "Moral Urgencies in the Nuclear Conflict," *Nuclear Weapons and the Conflict of Conscience,* ed. John C. Bennett (New York, 1962), p. 96.
[61] *FPCP*, p. 28.

not sanguine about his chances of success in that endeavor.[62]

Evidently Bennett's decision to advocate policies other than pacifism rests on judgments that these other policies will produce less harmful results than pacifism. Christian judgments about foreign policy must be framed with reference to certain good or bad consequences that the policies may have. Consequently, in order to investigate the actual policy guidelines, or middle axioms, Bennett has advocated since the Second World War, one must know what he understands the threats to human welfare to have been in that period.

The most commonly acknowledged threat, at least in the United States, is the tyranny associated with international Communism. However unfortunate the Communist ideology is, Bennett insists that one must distinguish between that ideology and the nations that embody it. Thus one's judgment about the reprehensibility of the ideology does not settle the question of the danger posed by nations espousing it. We will take up these questions in turn.

Bennett's rejection of Communism as a socio-economic ideology reveals clearly both his own political locus on the moderate Left and his use of judgments made by the World Council of Churches. Early in his career Bennett thought that the cure for the evils of the present economic system was socialism of some form. The socialism he espoused would not produce an equal financial reward for every man or a leveling down of achievement.[63] Rather socialism provided a way of correcting the great inequalities in the present (1931) private property system and of introducing an economic system that would be based on higher motives than the selfish seeking of profit.[64]

On the other hand, the socialist movement needed Christianity so as not to lose "appreciation of the value of the individual" person, so as not to become too materialistic, and

[62] FPCP, pp. 111–112.

[63] Bennett, "Myth Equal Opportunity" (1930), p. 1309.

[64] Bennett, "Can Christianity and Socialism Make Terms?" in The Christian Century, XLVIII, Part 1 (March 11, 1931), p. 338.

so as to avoid preoccupation with the changing of institutions rather than individuals.[65] In sum:

Christianity and socialism need to influence one another if either is to be healthy. Christianity without socialism loses contact with the economic realities. It lacks ethical sharpness. It becomes a glow which covers up the ruthlessness of the economic struggle and the selfishness of privilege. But socialism without Christianity is in danger of becoming secular, hard and narrow, so concerned with the economic relationships of life that it loses sight of the less obvious but richer values.[66]

The capitalist system must go. In the name of great words such as liberty it was a façade which "carefully guards the liberty of the business man to buy and sell and invent and produce" without guarding the "security of the mass of the people."[67] The great disproportions of power associated with capitalism produced a climate of fear among the powerless. This fear encouraged conformity and discouraged action.[68] Furthermore, the inequality of wealth associated with capitalism was bad in itself.[69] So were the selfishness and deception it stimulated.[70]

Bennett wrote all these things before he went to the Oxford Conference of 1937. At Oxford he was Secretary of the Section on Church, Community and State in Relation to the Economic Order.[71] The section produced a report which noted that capitalism had treated labor as a commodity and assumed that a pre-established harmony of the interests of individuals would lead society to naturally seek social justice.[72] To reform this

[65] *Ibid.*, p. 339.
[66] *Ibid.*, p. 338.
[67] *SS*, pp. 26–27.
[68] *CAOW*, pp. 37–39.
[69] *CAOW*, pp. 35–36.
[70] *CAOW*, pp. 36–37.
[71] Joseph H. Oldman, ed., *The Oxford Conference* (Official Report), p. 275. Also in this remarkable group were Charles Clayton Morrison, Reinhold Niebuhr, Paul Tillich, John Baillie, V. A. Demant, T. S. Eliot, and R. H. Tawney.
[72] *Ibid.*, pp. 82–83.

system (or non-system) the report mentioned two proposals: social ownership of basic industries and natural resources or, second, heavy taxation and legislation to control private corporate bodies. But the section did not commit itself to either of these proposals.[73]

Perhaps the reservation of the Oxford Section with respect to committing itself to socialism impressed Bennett. In any event this writer can find no arguments for socialism *per se* in his writing after that conference. In fact the Second World War turned his interests elsewhere. By 1948, while still maintaining the validity of the Oxford criticisms of capitalism,[74] he was willing to list some advantages of capitalism. It takes seriously the problems of incentive, distribution of economic power, and the impersonal, mechanical character of some dimensions of market activity.[75]

Such was Bennett's mind when the Amsterdam Assembly of the World Council of Churches convened in late August 1948. Again, Bennett was Secretary of the Section dealing with intranational problems.[76] The document this Section produced was shorter than the comparable Oxford report, but it caused considerable controversy. Yet it is clear that the committee meant to stay in the middle of the road. After saying that justice in economic activities meant the subordination of those activities to social ends, the report went on to criticize both the socialization and the absolutization of existing property rights if they become panaceas.[77]

The report defined the ideal social arrangement as a "re-

---

[73] *Ibid.*, pp. 94–97.

[74] *CCT* (1948–62), pp. 142–143: I assume that the original edition of this book was written before the Amsterdam Conference because there is no mention of Amsterdam in the 1948 edition. The conference was held late in 1948—(August 22–September 4).

[75] *CCT* (1948–62), pp. 139–142.

[76] World Council of Churches, *Amsterdam*, p. 225. The Chairman of the Section was C. L. Patijn. There were three vice-chairmen: Sir Walter Moberly, A. J. Hamlet, and Y. Y. Tsu.

[77] *Ibid.*, pp. 76–77.

sponsible society,"[78] which it found to be absent in the contemporary world. Capitalism and Communism were both criticized.[79] They were compared and criticized as follows:

> The Christian Churches should reject the ideologies of both Communism and *laissez-faire* capitalism, and should seek to draw men away from the false assumption that these extremes are the only alternatives. Each has made promises which it could not redeem. Communist ideology puts the emphasis upon economic justice, and promises that freedom will come automatically after the completion of the revolution. Capitalism puts the emphasis upon freedom, and promises that justice will follow as a byproduct of free enterprise; that, too, is an ideology which has been proved false. It is the responsibility of Christians to seek new, creative solutions which never allow justice or freedom to destroy the other.[80]

Bennett spent considerable time and energy explaining what this meant and what it did not mean. He insisted that the report did not put capitalism and Communism on the same level. Whereas the criticisms of Communism pointed to "elements that are inherent in the contemporary Communist movement with its center in the Soviet Union," those of capitalism denoted "tendencies in capitalism, tendencies which can be modified."[81] Capitalism was more malleable and less thoroughly worthy of condemnation than Communism.

But he admitted that the report did criticize both "systems." Produced by an ecumenical body as it was, it could do nothing else. Anything further to the "right" or "left" that might have been included in the report would have destroyed the consensus.[82] The delegates did not mean to suggest any specific next-steps for particular countries; they merely wanted to indicate criteria for the direction in which society should move.[83]

[78] *Ibid.,* pp. 77–78.
[79] *Ibid.,* p. 79.
[80] *Ibid.,* p. 80.
[81] Bennett, "Capitalism and Communism at Amsterdam" in *The Christian Century,* LXV (December 13, 1948), p. 1363.
[82] *Ibid.*
[83] *Ibid.,* p. 1364.

Therefore the report's wording must be carefully studied. Capitalism and Communism were not criticized as economic systems but as ideologies.[84]

In America capitalism tends to become an ideology vulnerable to the criticisms made at Oxford and Amsterdam.[85] For Europeans the word *capitalism* denotes a spiritual phenomenon —a bourgeois and individualistic culture. This is what is too prevalent in America and what Amsterdam found worthy of condemnation. Amsterdam did not mean to criticize an external, institutional market system.[86]

If the "responsible society" stands in judgment not so much over the concept of a plurality of centers of economic power and the importance of a market system as it does over nonplanning and individualism, what forms might it take in actual society? One form was British socialism, but that was not the only form.[87] The important thing it called for was remaining open to new possibilities, to experimentation. The search for a "third way" was "based upon the assumption that no known economic system adequately serves all the values which an economic system should serve—productivity, justice, and freedom."[88] Something new must be found and to that end the church should be a "critic of the status quo in all situations."

At the time of the Evanston meeting of the World Council,[89] Bennett was still stressing the ambiguity of the word *capitalism*. To Americans it suggests an effective and modifiable economic system; to Europeans it suggests exploitation, individualism, and materialism; to Asians it suggests imperialism. A word this

[84] See above, chapters 1–3, and Bennett, "The Responsible Society" (1949), p. 324.

[85] Bennett, "Capitalism and Communism at Amsterdam" (1948), p. 1364; cf. *CCT* (1948–62), pp. 138–139.

[86] *Ibid.*, pp. 1362–1363.

[87] *Ibid.*, p. 1364.

[88] Bennett, "The Responsible Society" (1949), pp. 324–325.

[89] World Council of Churches, *Evanston Report*, p. 334; Bennett was a vice-chairman of Section III along with E. C. Sobrepena; C. L. Patijn was again chairman; Paul Abrecht was secretary; Charles C. West was liaison officer.

vague should not be used.[90] Evanston reflected a tendency in ecumenical circles since Amsterdam to "reject the idea that a consistent socialization of the economy would be an advance."[91] But Evanston did not back away from the thrust of the Amsterdam statement. While Communism (not capitalism) was criticized, anti-Communism was also repudiated.[92]

Since Evanston, Bennett's views on what a "responsible society" would involve have remained fairly constant. He remains convinced that free enterprise, while a good thing, is not to be absolutized. In order to discuss economic issues rationally, one must accept as a presupposition "the responsibility of the national state to act to prevent large scale unemployment and other national economic disasters, and to co-operate with the states in meeting many social needs such as the provision for social security and public housing."[93]

The state must take economic responsibility. Because of its centrality, administrative capacities, and power to coerce, it is "the only agency in the national community that can deal effectively with problems which affect the welfare of the whole nation." Further, although it is true that there are areas of social existence which the state should leave alone—aspects of family, religious and educational life—"this is not true of economic institutions to the same degree." There is no "inherent moral or social principle" which says that government economic action is wrong. State action in the economic sphere safeguards the freedom of the economically weak against their strong neighbors.

Some may say it would be better if people took care of the weak voluntarily, if there were no coercion involved. To this

[90] Bennett, " 'The Responsible Society' at Evanston" in *Christianity and Crisis,* XIV, No. 12 (July 12, 1954), p. 91; cf. among other places, Bennett, "Freedom and Justice" (1959), p. 333.

[91] Bennett, Editorial: "Evanston on the Economic Order" in *Christianity and Society,* XIX, No. 3 (1954), p. 4.

[92] World Council of Churches, *Evanston Report,* p. 113.

[93] *CS,* p. 117; cf. Bennett, "How My Mind Has Changed" (1959), pp. 1501–1502; Bennett, "Christian Ethics and Forms of Economic Power" (1954), p. 247.

one must respond that "it is morally better to decide that what is required to meet the needs of people be effectively done even though this may involve coercion . . . than it is to oppose such legal action so that one may have the experience of feeling more moral." Of course state economic action may, in theory, lead to totalitarianism, but, in fact, "the greatest danger of totalitarianism comes not from the gradual extension of the role of government but rather from the breakdown of a society partly because the government has been too weak to deal with its problems."[94]

Writing from this perspective, Bennett has found it impossible to regard Communist ideology as anathema. The ideology is mistaken but belief in it, and/or life in a nation ruled by those who do, is not the worst evil imaginable. What sort of threat is posed for non-Communists by such a nation?

With many other observers Bennett did not regard Russia as a serious threat in the years during and immediately after the close of the Second World War. Reacting to the "Moscow Declarations" of November 1, 1943, he argued that Russia had a "co-operative spirit," that the "specter of Russia seeking to dominate Europe single-handed" need no longer haunt Europeans. There had once been ground for distrusting Russia, he went on, but we now had "good reason to believe that distrust need not . . . control our relations with Russia."[95]

In 1945, while condemning current Russian methods, he suggested that the reader remember "other factors," such as the deep sense of insecurity of the Russian people, the non-Russian source of the tragedy in Eastern Europe, the absence of militarism from Russian culture, the welfare-seeking aspects of Communist philosophy, and the real moral health of the Russian people.[96] The Russian expansionist tendencies should be opposed, he said, primarily through the strengthening of the

[94] *CS*, pp. 117–122.

[95] Bennett, Editorial: "The New Hope and the New Unity" in *Christianity and Crisis*, III, No. 20 (November, 1943), p. 1.

[96] Bennett, Editorial: "America and Russia" in *Christianity and Crisis*, V, No. 21 (December 10, 1945), pp. 1–2.

non-Communist Left, and, at the same time, Russian fears of America and Britain must be alleviated.[97]

Events in the late 1940's and early 1950's modified his views. In an article entitled "Can We Ever Support Communism?" in 1952 he answered the question with a resounding "No." If the Christian had no political power at all:

... it would be better for him to support no political movement and to work in indirect ways through the Church for the development of the moral and spiritual conditions which in the future will be more favorable to an alternative, than to help Communism win power.[98]

This opposition to the tyrannous aspect of the political power of the Communist nations is something Bennett reaffirmed as late as the revised edition of *Christianity and Communism* in 1960. The horrors of Stalinism were not accidental, he argued, but were the result of the attempt of radical and rapid social reform. The Communist ideology is atheistic and formed by a naturalism contrary to the Christian understanding of man. The extension of this ideology and of Russian (or Chinese) power over other nations is to be resisted. This was especially important because there was no reason to think that the period of ruthless tyranny will not last indefinitely: "there is no structure within Communist government that can be depended on as a source of self-correction."[99]

Nevertheless, in that book, and as recently as 1966, Bennett has insisted that there are two aspects of the contemporary world that are too often overlooked. The first of these is the diminishing of a global and unified Communist threat to the free world. The Communists are by no means united, as can be seen in the Sino-Soviet split and the diversity within Eastern European Communism. Second, a gradual process of humaniza-

[97] Bennett, Editorial: "The Russian-Communist Drive for Power" in *Christianity and Crisis,* VI, No. 20 (November 25, 1946), pp. 1–2.

[98] Bennett, "Can We Ever Support Communism?" in *The Christian Century,* LXII (June 11, 1952), p. 697.

[99] *CCT* (1960–62), pp. 70–75; the quotation is from p. 74.

tion has taken place among the European Communist nations. There has been a significant growth of cultural freedom there. These are real changes in priorities, not simply changes in tactics.

Because these things are true, what is at stake in the Cold War is not permanent slavery. Our attitude toward nations which are now Communist should be one of sympathy not hostility. Communism is not always worse than civil war, anarchy, or neglect of social injustice. The rising generation of Marxist intellectuals should be listened to, and the spiritual conflict that remains should be separated from the political conflict.[100]

Thus our situation is quite different from what it was during the early 1940's. What is at stake is quite different. Communism is more open-ended, more changeable than was Naziism. While the Nazi ideology was reactionary in the extreme, Communism represents the perversion of basically good impulses. There are forms of social organization worse than Communism. Second, because Communism can improve some societies and because it makes an idealistic kind of appeal, the threat it poses is not primarily military. People are more likely to become Communists as a result of propaganda than as a result of conquest. Third, in the Second World War we were defending nations which had political stability and a desire to be independent. But in Asia, where Communism makes its greatest appeal today, these conditions are present to the same degree. Fourth, now all foreign policy decisions "must take account of the danger of nuclear war."[101]

While this book will not take up Professor Bennett's polemics

[100] *FPCP,* pp. 80–92. Since I have to summarize at this stage, it seems best to refer to a place where Bennett has summed up his views. Lest anyone think Bennett now means that Communist expansion is not to be opposed, he should consult *FPCP,* pp. 72–74 and 77.

[101] This breakdown is taken from Bennett's Editorial: "From Supporter of War in 1941 to Critic in 1966" in *Christianity and Crisis,* XXVI, No. 2 (February 21, 1966), pp. 13–14; cf. *CS,* p. 170.

on the Vietnamese War, it is important enough to stress, in passing, that his views on that conflict are the logical outgrowth of his understanding of the dynamics of Asian Communism— views he has held for at least nineteen years. This understanding is the result of trips to Asia in the late 1940's and early 1950's. In 1950 he said that "the only effective resistance to Communism [in Asia] is the effort to discover better solutions to the problems which give Communists their opportunity."[102] Against MacArthur: ". . . military power can do little to defend Asia from Communism, or to destroy it where it is in power. If Communism spreads far in Asia, it will be because of the disparate problems of Asian countries and not because of the strength of Communist armies."[103]

Too many Americans think of the containment of Communism in military terms. It is not that kind of problem in Asia. To stop Communism there we must correct poverty, landlordism, and corruption.[104] For Bennett, human welfare in Asia is not in general served by the use of military force. Therefore, when he opposes certain military policies in Vietnam, for example, it is not because he has lost his nerve in the face of the need to use force; it is because he does not think that force will work. If critics, or his own careless statements, sometimes suggest otherwise, they do him an injustice.

If Communism represents one (however often misunderstood) threat to human welfare in the affairs of nations, the existence of nuclear weapons poses the other. As early as 1952

[102] Bennett, "The Christian Answer to Communism" (1950), pp. 355–356.

[103] Bennett, Editorial: "The MacArthur Controversy" in *Christianity and Crisis*, XI, No. 8 (May 14, 1951), p. 58.

[104] See, for example, Bennett, "Has India an Alternative?" in *The Christian Century*, LXVIII (February 28, 1951), p. 266; Bennett, Editorial: "Europe Versus Asia" in *Christianity and Crisis*, XII, No. 16 (September 29, 1952), pp. 121–122; Bennett, Editorial: "Our Distorted View of Asia" in *Christianity and Crisis*, XV, No. 6 (April 18, 1955), pp. 41–42; Bennett, Editorial: "The U.S. and China" in *Christianity and Crisis*, XXV, No. 6 (April 19, 1965), pp. 74 and 76.

183

Bennett could insist that the braking of Communism and the prevention of general war represented two distinct foreign policy objectives.[105] These two objectives might sometimes conflict and if they do: "The prevention of war should have priority because a nuclear war has greater finality as a threat to humanity than Communism. Communism is not eternal. . . ."[106] The prevention of war should be a distinct, separate, and permanent policy objective.[107]

The existence of nuclear weapons increases the possibility of disharmony between these two objectives.[108] The classic way of reconciling them was to say that the possession of the power to go to war would prevent war from happening. But nuclear weapons are a unique kind of potential power. The ICBMs for instance "put a terrible premium on being the first to strike and there is a great danger that . . . one nation may strike first in the fear that its opponent is about to attack."[109] As weapons technology evolves one can be less and less certain that the possession of weapons will prevent war. If the nuclear arms race continues, it will be more and more easy for nuclear war to start accidentally.[110] Thus we face what Bennett calls the "nuclear dilemma":

One side of this dilemma is the implacability of the adversary and the threat that at last by blackmail his power may be extended unless he finds himself limited by unyielding force. But the other side of this dilemma can only be spelled out in terms of the human consequences of nuclear war, even of the nuclear arms race itself, and this cannot be done without raising the question of the degree

[105] Bennett, Editorial: "Two Goals in Foreign Policy" in *Christianity and Crisis*, XII, No. 8 (May 12, 1952), pp. 57–58.
[106] *CS*, pp. 188–189.
[107] Cf. Bennet, Editorial: "The Great Conflict of Opinion" in *Christianity and Crisis*, XIX, No. 8 (May 11, 1959), pp. 61–62; *CCT* (1960–62), p. 160.
[108] Bennett, Editorial: "The Atomic Bomb and the Future" in *Christianity and Crisis*, IX, No. 17 (October 7, 1949), pp. 129–130.
[109] *CS*, p. 172.
[110] Bennett, "Moral Urgencies" (1962), pp. 95–96.

184

of destruction a nuclear war might cause us to inflict on human beings in another nation.[111]

What are the consequences of maintaining a policy of nuclear deterrence? Americans tend to oversimplify them.

Bennett is set against the interpretation of the consequences of nuclear war as proposed, for example, by theorist Herman Kahn (in *On Thermonuclear War*). He believes that one cannot ignore, as Kahn does, such *qualitative* factors as the emotional health of people and their morale. Again, one has to realize, on the *quantitative* side, that an ideally organized civil defense system is both psychologically and politically impossible. Also, as more powerful weapons are built, more damage becomes possible. The loss of the leaders of a society will result in social breakdown that will have serious effects on those who remain.[112] We should stress the "intangible or qualitative consequences of nuclear war." It might be possible to take a large number of casualties for the sake of freedom—something men need very much—but "in all probability freedom would be a casualty of nuclear war for a longer time than it would be a casualty of Communist power."[113]

In a society spiritually, socially, and physically decimated the only viable form of social organization would be a dictatorship. The problems faced would be increased by the likelihood of genetic damage.[114] Thus it is hard to see how any calculation about what the world needs could justify the use of nuclear weapons.[115] For men to act so as to bring nearer the doom of the human race—as a thermonuclear war surely would—"is to be guilty of final disobedience to the God of life and love, and of ultimate treason to humanity."[116]

[111] Bennett, "Forward," *Nuclear Weapons and the Conflict of Conscience,* ed. John C. Bennett (New York, 1962), p. 10; *FPCP*, pp. 112–116.
[112] Bennett, "Moral Urgencies" (1962), pp. 97–100.
[113] Bennett, "Moral Tensions" (1964), p. 23.
[114] Bennett, "Moral Urgencies" (1962), pp. 105–108.
[115] *WCMPD*, pp. 83ff.; *FPCP*, p. 103.
[116] *FPCP*, pp. 105–107.

185

The fact that we can entertain the possibility of committing such an atrocity is a result of the "deterioration of our moral judgment" which occurred during the Second World War. At that time we allowed our military leaders to engage in unjustifiable acts "under the pressure of war."[117] We "assumed that any degree of violence was permitted if it made victory more likely."[118] We experienced a kind of "corporate fall" and seemed to say that "there are no limits to the violence that is permitted against the enemy at a distance."[119] This erosion of our moral fiber has ill-prepared us, Bennett thinks, for our responsibilities today.

In fact the actual existence of the dilemma weakens our fiber still further.

Have we even begun to consider the spiritual effect upon nations and churches if we live for decades with the assumption that at any moment we may be destroyed while we let loose the forces of destruction on scores of millions of our neighbors?[120]

As we constantly threaten to use nuclear weapons our inhibitions against using them are undermined. Preoccupation with civil defense makes our culture morbid and insecure. Too much power shifts into the hands of the military; we become a garrison state.[121]

What should be done to get us out of this situation? The common welfare will be enhanced if two things are done.

First, we should make clear that we will not be the first to use nuclear weapons. In 1954 Bennett wrote, ". . . it is doubtful if our consciences have been toughened enough even in these tough times to approve of the destruction of several million people by one such deed unless we had first been at-

---

[117] Bennett, "Moral Urgencies" (1962), pp. 101–105.
[118] Bennett, "Moral Tensions" (1964), p. 22.
[119] *WCMPD,* pp. 78–80.
[120] Bennett, "The World in Which We Live" in *The Congregational Quarterly,* XXVI (1958), p. 213.
[121] Bennett, "Moral Urgencies" (1962), pp. 109–112.

tacked by the same method."[122] By 1961 he had even more misgivings about use in retaliation, but he was still against our use of nuclear weapons first.[123] The basis for this refusal is the real line—psychological as it may be—which can be drawn between nuclear weapons and weapons of other kinds. Refusal to escalate a conflict into the nuclear stage is to stop at a recognizable threshold. Therefore we should absolutely refuse to be the first to use tactical or strategic nuclear weapons.[124]

Early in his confrontation with the nuclear dilemma Bennett insisted that our refusal to be the first to use nuclear weapons should be a matter of public record. It should be our *announced* policy.[125] The trouble with this view, of course, is that making the announcement undercuts the deterrent value of the possession of nuclear weapons:

Under present circumstances, if we announced our intention never to use thermonuclear weapons, we could invite precisely the consequences Dr. Bennett most fears. For the one lesson of the Cold War is that Soviet advances have been checked only through the use of countervailing power—with power being defined in broad moral and material as well as military terms. If we announce when and how we will use or not use the power available to us—if the past is any guide—the Soviets will move to exploit our declaration.[126]

Bennett took this with some seriousness but remained unconvinced. He was, he said, "inconsistent enough to be willing to take advantage of the fact that the Government does not show its hand in the present situation." Yet the church should not

[122] Bennett, Editorial: "A New Dimension of Moral Perplexity" in *Christianity and Crisis*, XIV, No. 7 (May 3, 1954), pp. 49–50.

[123] Bennett, *et al.*, "The Nuclear Dilemma—A Discussion" in *Christianity and Crisis*, XXI, No. 19 (November 13, 1961), p. 200.

[124] *FPCP*, pp. 124–126.

[125] Bennett, Editorial: "The Atomic Bomb" (1949), pp. 129–130; cf. Bennett, Editorial: "Conscience and the H-Bomb" in *Christianity and Crisis*, XVI, No. 20 (November 26, 1956), pp. 157–158.

[126] Kenneth W. Thompson in Bennett, *et al.*, "The Nuclear Dilemma —A Discussion" (1961), p. 203.

187

keep silent in a situation in which some were advocating the first use of nuclears.[127] Responding to critics who said we should not have revealed that we would not have used force in the Cuban crisis in 1962, he noted that citizens and the churches must encourage the government to renounce first use since the more belligerent elements in the country are not silent and our moral restraint was reassuring to those in many parts of the world. There was a difference of roles.

> The Churches and individual citizens perhaps have a different role from that of the President and his advisors. The latter should not be asked to agonize in public, and it may be that good results come from the fact that our officials let the impression stand that we were about to attack Cuba.[128]

The churches, at least, had to cry out against an attitude that would justify first use of nuclear weapons.[129]

This suggests Bennett's most recent position. He has not demanded that the nation publicly commit itself. The credibility of the nuclear deterrent depends on our not giving the impression that we would never use nuclear weapons.[130] We should "for the present" take advantage of the uncertainty created by our government's silence on this matter.[131] And, by 1966, he was saying that if some nuclear weapons can be used for legitimate as well as illegitimate purposes, and if possession of them is the surest way to prevent war, then "at least to create enough uncertainty as to whether they might be used, for them to act as a deterrent . . . may be a service to the neighbor."[132] Our government should be dedicated to the repudiation of first

---

[127] Bennett, "The Nuclear Discussion—Continued" in *Christianity and Crisis,* XXI, No. 21 (December 11, 1961), pp. 223–224.

[128] Bennett, Editorial: "Ethics and Tactics in a Crisis" in *Christianity and Crisis,* XXII, No. 21 (December 10, 1962) pp. 222–223.

[129] *WCMPD,* pp. 80–81.

[130] Bennett, "Christian Ethics and International Affairs" in *Christianity and Crisis,* XXIII, No. 14 (August 5, 1963), p. 150.

[131] Bennett, "Moral Tensions" (1964), pp. 23–25.

[132] Bennett, *et al., The Road to Peace* (1966), pp. 39–40.

use of nuclears, but its announcement of that dedication, a distinct act, is probably wrong.

The second thing that we should do so as to serve human welfare in the nuclear age is to reject the idea that one target is as good as another. We should say that we will not strike at population centers with our weapons—nuclear or non-nuclear.

Some of Bennett's agonizing over this point may come from the fact that he feels he did not take a strong enough stand against some actions by our military forces in World War II. In 1945 he signed an editorial which while it was clearly against indiscriminate and unrestricted bombing accepted "the bombing of strategic centers and objects as a doleful necessity of modern war. . . ."[133] But in an interesting autobiographical reflection in 1946 he said:

I could never dispel the suspicion that if I had been an eyewitness of the effects of the bombing . . . I would have been forced to say that—whatever arguments might be brought forth—these deeds are so evil, so utterly abhorrent to the conscience of any Christian who really knows in detail their human consequences, that they must be rejected. Since the war ended and the full human effects of this obliteration bombing have become known this suspicion has been confirmed.[134]

Bennett began to reject the bombing of cities when he began to be able to assess the consequences of that action.

This suggests the difference between the justification he gives for the prohibition of attack on civilians from the justification given by Professor Paul Ramsey. Ramsey, in his many writings on this subject, argues that war as a form of human activity is justifiable only as an act of service to some neighbors. One can justify the killing of men who, because of their social function, threaten the welfare of other neighbors. But this is a justification for killing only men engaged in that function. Consequently the justification of waging war does not justify directly

[133] *Christianity and Crisis,* V, No. 11 (June 25, 1945), p. 1.
[134] *CESP,* p. 20.

killing those who are noncombatants in the war. A so-called act of war is reprehensible, in Ramsey's terms, if one knows "that there are civilians whose lives are made the *intended, direct* object of violence. . . ."[135] Ramsey's decision about acts directed against populations is not based on an assessment of the damage that such an act might do (or, of its consequences) but on a prior analysis of what kinds of acts of killing can be legitimate. His decision is not revisable in the light of the act's consequences.

Bennett finds this formalism abhorrent. Ramsey's view, it seems to him, tacitly justifies the killing of vast numbers of people so long as one means well. Therefore, "it is useful to be guided not only by intention but also by a realistic view of the total consequences of an attack." One should strike at soldiers rather than at civilians not because they are for some reason more legitimate targets, but "because such repression is the direct way to reduce violence."[136] How can Ramsey justify this "functional" distinction between combatants and non-combatants? He overemphasizes it.[137] He has constructed a theory which allows him to leave out of account the extent of the evil involved in the annihilation of combatants:

If a neutron bomb or some other type of nuclear weapon were used to destroy the whole military personnel, leaving buildings and weapons intact, and if this were done in the fighting of a limited war, I should hope that Ramsey would not think that the moral problem of "limited war" had been solved.[138]

The point for Bennett is that a decision about the legitimacy of a form of military action must be justified in terms of its

[135] This formulation is taken from Paul Ramsey, "The Case for Making 'Just War' Possible," *Nuclear Weapons and the Conflict of Conscience*, ed. John C. Bennett (New York, 1962), pp. 144–159; the quotation is from p. 153.

[136] Bennett, "Moral Urgencies" (1962), pp. 104–105.

[137] Bennett, "Moral Tensions" (1964), p. 22.

[138] Bennett, "The Debate on the Nuclear Dilemma" in *Theology Today*, XVIII, No. 4 (January, 1962), p. 417.

consequences—in terms of its effect on human welfare. Ramsey's attempt to justify it on other grounds forces him to ask about the "intention" of an action and to permit an action on that uncertain basis quite apart from its "collateral damage." This raises the danger that the criteria by which one assesses intention will be too subjective and "that almost any destruction will be permitted if it is not intended."[139] Ramsey's preoccupation with justification of a class of acts in principle makes it hard for him to assess specific acts in fact.

Rather, there should be a prohibition on attacking cities because that attack has terrible consequences. Ramsey should admit that it is possible that an action which has a justifiable "intention" may have unjustifiable consequences. If he did that, he would be forced to realize that the more sober course is to stick to the assessment of consequences. What Bennett wants to emphasize is "not the distinction between combatant and noncombatants . . . but the fact that indiscriminate warfare destroys the fabric of the community and its capacity for recuperation." His concern with the problem of the safety of populations is expressed more in terms of the "principle of proportion" than anything else.[140] Therefore, what he really defends is the principle that:

. . . any strategies that have as their effect the destruction of populations *on a large scale* and that render another nation unable to recover are murderous, out of all bounds theologically and morally, incapable of justification by any political calculation.[141]

The extent to which these criticisms are fair to Ramsey's views—especially since he has begun to stress the role of the principle of proportion—are not the concern of this book. What is of interest is Bennett's consistent insistence that a justifiable act of war must be one which does only a justifiable

[139] *FPCP*, p. 120.
[140] Bennett, *et al.*, *The Road to Peace* (1966), pp. 36–37.
[141] *FPCP*, p. 122, emphasis added.

191

amount of damage. The amount of damage should be proportionate to the cause at stake. Since today the cause is limited, the damage inflicted should be limited. As Bennett rightly says, this is a concept of *limited,* not of *just,* war.[142]

John Bennett's reflections on foreign policy are, in a sense, a fitting place to end exposition of his thought. They represent a forum in which one sees not only his changes of mind and the changing world in which he lived, but one in which his heartfelt concerns come to the surface. For almost forty years he has insisted that American sensitivity to human need should be attuned to men in other lands—an insistence expressed in literally hundreds of editorials, articles and books.

We have seen, moreover, that Bennett's thought and comment over thirty-nine years manifest continuity of concern, emphasis, and vocabulary. Amid Bennett's diverse writings there are certain concepts—need, welfare, perspective, translation, consensus—which he has used in characteristic and discernible ways. He has articulated these concepts into an often implicit system of thought which manifests a remarkable degree of internal consistency.

There are some other gratifying strengths of Bennett's thought. He is able to assert the relevance of Christian concepts to political life without making religious ideas inflexible or political thought and judgment of secondary status. His theology is radically undogmatic; his social concern radically uninhibited. Yet his religious views and loyalties always inform his social judgments. His understanding of the basis of theology in experience, his doctrines of God and man, his view of the church and God's commands all suggest that Christianity requires social action and involvement, and action and involvement of a rather definite kind, without implicitly closing the mind of the Christian to new theological concepts or new social facts.

[142] *WCMPD,* pp. 75 and 85–88; cf. CS, p. 163.

Not only is Bennett's thought a statement of a plausible understanding of the relation of religious to political ideas, it is as a whole a remarkably open system. For Bennett irenicism becomes a systematic principle to such an extent that it is easy for his own characteristic ideas to go unnoticed. When Professor Bennett wants to establish a point he instinctively asserts that many people (preferably theologians, ideally the World Council of Churches) have made the same claim. His desire to see some good in everything has, as a systematic correlate, the concept of consensus. There is both an ecclesiastical and a national consensus. Because a consensus is important Bennett must remain open to new ideas; when a consensus exists, it provides a basis for criticism of some developments.

Furthermore, Bennett's irenicism makes his theology an unusually good reflection of the experience of his generation of theologians. *On the basis of his own convictions* his systematic objective has been to discover those things on which he and his contemporaries could agree. He has held that it was theologically important to distill and clarify that agreement; his success has not gone unnoticed.[143]

Once this is said (and of course I have only suggested some general strengths of Bennett's work) we may recall that there are points at which his thought is weak on its own terms or productive of consequences he, or someone else, might find unfortunate. These points characteristically cluster around the role Bennett assigns the church in society. Despite these problems, we can say that the achievement of John C. Bennett has been considerable. The difficulties of his thought are difficulties which occurred precisely because he was vividly aware of the weak spots in the theories of his contemporaries. He tried to compensate for those weaknesses and, in the process, produced a body of thought which is itself vulnerable to criticism.

Bennett is, at the same time, the first Niebuhrian and a man with different concerns than his more famous colleague. Both

[143] See, for example, Reinhold Niebuhr, Review of *CESP* in *Christianity and Society*, XII, No. 1 (Winter, 1946), p. 41.

men insisted on a reformation in theology and politics; both justified this insistence by an appeal to experience. But, for Bennett, what matters most is not a consistent theory, but the establishment of a social process by which the *church* can consistently serve as a prophetic critic. Contributing to this process, raising the level of the consensus, modestly but eloquently expressing the judgments of the church in his time—these are the greatest achievements of John C. Bennett.

The Works of John C. Bennett

BOOKS

Social Salvation: A Religious Approach to the Problems of Social Change. New York, 1935. Reissued with a new preface (1946) in an edition dated 1948.

Christianity—And Our World. New York, 1936. One of the Hazen books on Religion.

Christian Realism. New York, 1941. Reissued without change in 1952.

Christian Ethics and Social Policy. New York, 1946. Reissued without change in 1956.

Christianity and Communism. New York, 1946. Amended and republished as *Christianity and Communism Today* in 1960; further additions in 1962.

Christian Social Action. London, 1954. This is an English edition of *Christian Ethics and Social Policy.*

Christian Values and Economic Life, with Howard R. Bowen, William A. Brown Jr., and G. Bromley Oxnam. New York, 1954.

The Christian as Citizen. London, 1955. World Christian Books No. 5.

Christians and the State. New York, 1958.

Christian Faith and Political Change. Toronto, 1963. Contains the first three chapters of *When Christians Make Political Decisions.*

When Christians Make Political Decisions. New York, 1964.

Foreign Policy in Christian Perspective. New York, 1966.

BOOKS EDITED BY BENNETT

Nuclear Weapons and the Conflict of Conscience. New York, 1962.
Christian Social Ethics in a Changing World. New York, 1966.

SHORTER ESSAYS

These are to be distinguished from books on the one hand and from editorials and book reviews on the other. Some pieces are articles in journals, some are contributions to symposia, and others are pamphlets.

The following list is a selection, not a complete bibliography. An approximately complete bibliography through 1967 is contained in the author's doctoral thesis, on file in the Princeton University Library.

"The Myth of Equal Opportunity" in *The Christian Century*, XLVII (October 29, 1930), pp. 1308–1309.

"Can Armistice Sunday be Saved?" in *The Christian Century*, XLVII (November 26, 1930), pp. 1444–1445.

"Can Christianity and Socialism Make Terms?" in *The Christian Century*, XLVIII (March 11, 1931), pp. 338–339.

"Christianity and Class-Consciousness in *Fellowship Leaflets #2*, Published by the FOR, 383 Bible House, NYC.

"Christianity and Class-Consciousness" in *The World Tomorrow*, XV (February, 1932), pp. 47–49; the original locus of the essay in the above pamphlet.

"Religion: Opiate or Stimulant" in *The World Tomorrow*, XV (June, 1932), pp. 178–180.

"After Liberalism—What?" in *The Christian Century*, L (November 8, 1933), pp. 1403–1406.

"That Fellowship Questionnaire" in *The World Tomorrow*, XVI (December 21, 1933), pp. 690–692.

"Calling for a New United Front" in *The World Tomorrow*, XVII (January 4, 1934), pp. 21–22; this is a letter to the editor.

"The Relevance of the Ethic of Jesus for Modern Society" in *Religion in Life*, III, No. 1 (1934), pp. 74–83.

"The World Needs the Church" in *The Younger Churchmen Look at the Church*, ed. Ralph Read (New York, 1935), pp. 15–32.

"Moral Landmarks in a Time of Confusion" in *Christendom*, I, No. 1 (Autumn, 1935), pp. 67–78.

"The Religious Foundations for Social Education and Action," the first of a series of Social Progress Pamphlets, published by the Department of Social Education and Action, Board of Christian Education, The Presbyterian Church in the U.S.A., 1937, 26 pp.

"The Contribution of Reinhold Niebuhr" in *Religion in Life*, VI, No. 2 (1937), pp. 268–283.

"Christianity and Social Salvation," a pamphlet published by the Board of Christian Education of the Presbyterian Church in the U. S. A., Philadelphia, 1938, 15 pp.

"The Causes of Social Evil" in *Christian Faith and the Common Life* (Church, Community and State Series), London, 1938, pp. 173–196.

"New Emphases in Christian Social Teaching" in *The Church Faces the World: Studies in Preparation for the Madras Conference of the International Missionary Council*, ed. Samuel McCrea Cavert (New York, 1939), pp. 1–18.

"A Changed Liberal—But Still a Liberal" in *The Christian Century*, LVI (February 8, 1939), pp. 179–181.

"Neutrality: The Christian's Dilemma" in *The Christian Century*, LVI (November 1, 1939), pp. 1329–1331.

"Christianity and Democracy: A Study of Relationship" in *Christendom*, V, No. 2 (Spring, 1940), pp. 162–171.

"The Christian's Ethical Decision" in *Religion in Life*, IX (Summer, 1940), pp. 393–401.

"From One Illusion to Another" in *The Christian Century*, LVII (September 18, 1940), pp. 1146–1147; a letter to the editor —the title is obviously not Bennett's.

"If America Enters the War" in *The Christian Century*, LVII (December 4, 1940), pp. 1506–1508.

"Christian Faith and Political Strategy" in *Christianity and Crisis*, I, No. 2 (February 24, 1941), pp. 3–6.

"Christianity and Its Alternatives" in *Christendom*, VI, No. 3 (1941), pp. 352–363.

"Not a Holy War" in *The Christian Century*, LVIII (October 8, 1941), pp. 1243–1244; a letter to the editor.

"The Outlook for Theology" in *The Journal of Religion*, XXI, No. 4 (October, 1941), pp. 341–353.

"Revolution or Counter-Revolution?" in *The Christian Century*, LIX (February 18, 1942), pp. 209–211.

"In Such a Time" in *Christendom*, VII, No. 2 (1942), pp. 162–168.

"The Christian Conception of Man" in *Liberal Theology: An Appraisal—Essays in Honor of Eugene William Lyman*, eds. Henry P. Van Dusen and David E. Roberts (New York, 1942), pp. 191–204.

"Enduring Bases of Christian Action" in *Social Action*, IX, No. 6 (June 15, 1943), pp. 5–34.

"The Person of Christ" in *Religion in Life*, XII, No. 4 (1943), pp. 503–513.

"Inaugural Address," as a member of the Union Theological Seminary faculty, in *The Union Theological Seminary Alumni Bulletin*, XIX, No. 1 (December, 1943), pp. 2–6; given September 29, 1943.

"The Hardest Problem for Christian Ethics" in *Christianity and the Contemporary Scene*, eds. Randolph C. Miller and Henry H. Shires (New York, 1943), pp. 119–130.

"The Christian Basis for Enduring Peace" in *Approaches to World Peace*, eds. Lyman Bryson *et al.* (New York, 1944), pp. 750–754; for comments see pp. 754–762.

"The Protestant Churches and World Order" in *World Order: Its Intellectual and Cultural Foundations*, ed. F. Ernest Johnson (New York, 1945), pp. 124–136.

"The Meaning of Redemption in Personal and Social Life Today" in *The Journal of Religious Thought*, III, No. 1 (Autumn, Winter, 1946), pp. 54–62.

"The Forms of Ecumenical Christianity" in *Toward World-Wide Christianity*, ed. O. Frederick Nolde (New York, 1946), pp. 59–77 (The Interseminary Series, Volume IV).

"The Limitations of the Church" in *The Gospel, the Church, and the World,* ed. Kenneth Scott Latourette (New York, 1946), pp. 134–156 (The Interseminary Series, Volume III).

"The Involvement of the Church" in World Council of Churches, *The Church and the Disorder of Society* (London, 1948), pp. 91–102.

"Modern Protestantism and Democracy" in *Review of Religion,* January, 1948, pp. 166–178.

"Comment" in *Christendom,* XIII, No. 1 (1948), pp. 55–57, a response to Peter Bertocci.

"Capitalism and Communism at Amsterdam" in *The Christian Century,* LXV (December 13, 1948), pp. 1362–1364.

"Supplement to 'The Christian Basis for Enduring Peace' " in *Perspectives on a Troubled Decade: Science, Philosophy and Religion 1939–1949,* eds. Lyman Bryson *et al.* (New York, 1950), pp. 695–701.

"A Christian View of the State" in *Journal of Religious Thought,* VIII (1951), pp. 105–113.

"A Protestant Conception of Religious Authority" in *The Union Seminary Quarterly Review,* VIII, No. 1 (November, 1951), pp. 3–10; reprinted later in *The Protestant Credo,* ed. Vergilius Ferm, 1953.

"The Church Between East and West" in *Christian Faith and Social Action,* ed. John Hutchison (New York, 1953).

"A Theological Conception of Goals for Economic Life" in *Goals of Economic Life,* ed. Alfred Dudley Ward (New York, 1953), pp. 397–429.

"A Protestant Conception of Religious Authority" in *The Protestant Credo,* ed. Vergilius Ferm (New York, 1953), pp. 127–138; this appeared in *The Union Seminary Quarterly* in 1951.

"The Church as Prophetic Critic" in *The Christian Century,* LXXI (January 6, 1954), pp. 9–11; reprinted in *The Christian Century Reader,* eds. Harold E. Fey and Margaret Frakes (New York, 1962), pp. 47–53 and in *Best Sermons (1955),* ed. G. Paul Butler (New York, 1955), pp. 277–285.

"Billy Graham at Union" in *The Union Seminary Quarterly Review,* IX, No. 4 (May 1954), pp. 9–14.

"Preface," "Christian Ethics and Economic Life," and "Christian

199

Ethics and Forms of Economic Power" in John Bennett *et al.,* *Christian Values and Economic Life* (New York, 1954).

"Christianity in its Political Setting" in *Religion in Life,* XXIV, No. 1 (1955), pp. 5–16; see following entry.

"Are There Tests of Revelation?" in *Theology Today,* XII, No. 1 (April, 1955), pp. 68–84.

"Notes on Christian Responsibility and National Interest" in *Christianity and Crisis,* XVI, No. 13 (July 23, 1956), pp. 100–101.

"Reinhold Niebuhr's Social Ethics" in *Reinhold Niebuhr: His Religious, Social, and Political Thought,* eds. Charles W. Kegley and Robert W. Bretall (New York, 1956), pp. 46–77.

"Protestant Ethics and Population Control" in *Daedalus,* LXXXVIII, No. 3 (1959), pp. 454–459; see *The United Church Herald,* II, No. 16 (September 3, 1959), pp. 4–6.

"The Demand for Freedom and Justice in the Contemporary World Revolution" in *Religion and Culture, Essays in Honor of Paul Tillich,* ed. Walter Leibrecht (New York, 1959), pp. 321–334.

"How My Mind Has Changed" in *The Christian Century,* LXVI (December 23, 1959), pp. 1500–1502; also in *How My Mind Has Changed,* ed. Harold E. Fey (Cleveland, 1961).

"The Kingdom of God" in *Christianity and Crisis,* XV, No. 10 (June 13, 1960), pp. 85–88.

"Christ and the Non-Christian" in *Christianity and Crisis,* XXI, No. 8 (May 15, 1961), pp. 73–76.

"The Nuclear Dilemma—A Discussion" in *Christianity and Crisis,* XXI, No. 19 (November 13, 1961), pp. 200–202; included in *Witness to a Generation,* ed. Wayne H. Cowan (New York, 1966), pp. 253ff.; see 1962.

"Christian Ethics and Political Decision: How Relevant are Universal Principles to Concrete Situation?" in *Worldview,* V, No. 2 (February, 1962), pp. 3–7; this is a slightly shortened version of "Principles and the Context" (1961).

"Christian Ethics and Foreign Policy" in *Catholic Mind,* LX, No. 1161 (March, 1962), pp. 13–25.

"Forward" and "Moral Urgencies in the Nuclear Conflict" in *Nuclear Weapons and the Conflict of Conscience,* ed. John C. Bennett (New York, 1962), pp. 7–12, 93–120.

"Reinhold Niebuhr's Contribution to Christian Social Ethics" in
Reinhold Niebuhr: A Prophetic Voice in Our Time, ed.
Harold R. Landon (Greenwich, Connecticut, 1962), 57–95.

"Church and State" in *New Frontiers of Christianity,* ed. Ralph
C. Raughley (New York, 1962), pp. 174–200.

"State Aid and the Church-Related College" in *Christianity and
Crisis,* XXIII, No. 6 (April 15, 1963), pp. 56–59; this also
appears in *Liberal Education.*

"Change and Continuity in the Theological Climate at Union
Seminary" in *The Union Seminary Quarterly Review,* XVIII,
No. 4 (May, 1963), pp. 357–367; a fascinating article occa-
sioned by President Van Dusen's retirement.

"The Religious Concern With Politics," a pamphlet published by
the National Conference of Christians and Jews, New York,
1963.

"Christianity and Secularist Humanism" in *Christianity on the
March,* ed. Henry P. Van Dusen (New York, 1963), pp.
127–147.

"A Protestant View of Authority in the Church" in *Theology
Digest* (Winter, 1963–1964), pp. 209–219.

"Inaugural Address as President of Union Seminary" in *The Union
Seminary Quarterly Review,* XIX, No. 4, part ii (May, 1964),
pp. 397–408; Address delivered April 10, 1964.

"Christian Ethics and the National Conscience," The Sixth Annual
Alexander Graham Bell Lectures on "Man's Communication
to Man," pamphlet, Boston, 1964.

"Moral Tensions in International Affairs," a pamphlet published
by the Council on Religion and International Affairs, 1964.

"Christian Ethics and Current Issues," a pamphlet containing the
M. T. Burt Lectures at the Cotner School of Religion,
Lincoln, Nebraska.

"In Defence of God" in *Look* (April 19, 1966), pp. 69–71;
since reprinted in *Radical Theology: Phase Two, Essays on the
Current Debate,* eds. C. W. Christian and Glenn R. Wittig
(Philadelphia, 1967), pp. 141–151.

"The Issue of Peace; the Voice of Religion" in *Worldview,* IX,
No. 4 (April, 1966), pp. 4–9.

"The Church and the Secular" in *Christianity and Crisis,* XXVI,
No. 22 (December 26, 1966), pp. 294–296; this also appears

in *The Princeton Seminary Bulletin,* LX, No. 1 (October, 1966), pp. 4–10.

"The Road to Peace: Christian Approaches to Defence and Disarmament," Philadelphia, 1966. Facet Books, Social Ethics Series No. 10; Bennett's essay is on pp. 32–41.

"Authority in Christian Social Ethics," the first of an unpublished series of Earl Lectures delivered January 31, 1967; mimeographed.

"The Protestant Ethic and Capitalism" in *Christianity and Crisis,* XXVII, No. 5 (April 3, 1967), pp. 64–68.

INDEX

Adams, James L., 154 n.76

Baillie, John, 175 n. 71
Barth, Karl, 10, 74, 145; "Barthians," 18
Berdyaev, Nicholas, 42
Bertocci, Peter, 151f.
Bonhoeffer, Dietrich, 74
Brunner, Emil, 10, 32, 76 n. 23

Christianity and other religions, 24–29
Communism, 24–26, 39–40, 63, 106, 135, 174–183
Consensus, national or moral, 81–85, 96f., 138; religious, 30f., 91–106, 145, 177
Contextualists, 73–79

Demant, V. A., 175 n. 71
Direct versus indirect action, 108f.

Eliot, Thomas S., 175 n. 71
Equality, 139

Faith and reason, 18–21
Fletcher, Joseph, 76–79, 82 n. 35
Freedom, 133–135

God, creator, 39–40; Lord of history, 41–43; provider of salvation, 43–47; righteous, 40–41
Graham, Billy, 18 n. 7

Hazelton, Roger, 61 n. 48
Heimann, Eduard, 129 n. 76, 135f., 140 n. 24
von Hügel, Baron Friedrich, 51 n. 15
Humility, 58–61

Jesus, and church, 53, 88f.; ethical teaching, 54–69; his divinity, 48–54
Johnson, F. Ernest, 112, 113 n. 21, 116f., 128 n. 73
Justice, 136–139

Kahn, Herman, 185
Koinonia, 74

Love, 61–69, 149f., 171; and justice, 71f., 137f.
Lehmann, Paul, 74, 152, 153 n. 75

McConnell, Francis J., 107
Meyer, Donald, 162 n. 14, 164 n. 20
Middle axioms, 140–155
Morrison, Charles Clayton, 101f., 104 n. 59, 163, 167f., 175 n. 71

203